FREEDOM & EVIL

FREEDOM & EVIL
A PILGRIM'S GUIDE TO HELL

GEORGE F. DOLE

**SWEDENBORG
FOUNDATION**
West Chester, Pennsylvania

Second printing, 2018

Library of Congress Cataloging-in-Publication Data

Dole, George F.
    Freedom and evil : A pilgrim s guide to hell / George F. Dole.
        p.   cm.
    Includes bibliographical references.
    ISBN 0-87785-399-1 (pbk.)
        1. Hell.   I. Title

BT836.2. D65 2001
236′.25–dc21

                                                                00–052310

Edited by Mary Lou Bertucci
Design and typesetting by Karen Connor

Cover image inspired by the artists from prrints.com.

Indo Apple image from the U.S. Department of Agriculture Pomological Watercolor Collection. Rare and Special Collections, National Agricultural Library, Beltsville, MD 20705.

Printed in the United States of America.

Swedenborg Foundation
320 North Church Street
West Chester, PA 19380
swedenborg.com

contents

To Mikhail Kazachkov,
with growing gratitude

introduction

One of the water routes from Bath to Boothbay Harbor in Maine takes you through the Upper and Lower Hellgates, constricted passages where current and tide meet with particular intensity. When you feel a ninety-foot excursion boat list, you realize that the smooth eddies on the surface only hint at the forces involved. I have a sense that in our own times, materialism and spirituality are meeting like current and tide and that the specific topic of hell is one of those constricted spaces where the encounter comes to particularly sharp focus.

Let us look first at the tide and the current and then at the restricted space. By "materialism" I mean the belief that nothing but matter is real or has real existence. Such immaterial experiences as ideas and feelings are no more than byproducts of physical events. Ideas are patterns of neural activity in the brain. Feelings are chemical reactions in the gastrointestinal tract. Notions of a human soul are superstitions left over from a prescientific past.

"Spirituality," on the contrary, takes thoughts and feelings with full seriousness. It often centers in a quest for meaning, which cannot be weighed or measured or in any sense quantified but which is held to be of paramount importance for human life and living. It may range from consciously held and clearly articulated religious beliefs in God to a vague sense that "there has to be more to life than this."

I read laments from time to time about "the rising tide of materialism"; but, on closer inspection, it seems that both materialism and spirituality are alive and well and living in America. The same decade that saw immense progress in the gene-mapping project saw an explosion of interest in angels. While we watched the space shuttle blasting off from Cape Canaveral, we read books about near-death experiences. I find it telling that advertisements for the latest, most advanced medicines appeal to longings for health and youth and beauty more than to scientific explanation of their benefits. *Why* we buy them seems disconnected from *how* they work, with each effective in its own realm and quite powerless in the other. Indeed, we will see throughout this book a persistent contrast between *why* and *how*.

It will very soon become obvious that I find strict materialism wholly inadequate as an account of the world I live in. In late nineteenth-century America, there was a wave of belief that technology—electricity, in particular—was going to make poverty and misery things of the past. We have made immense technological strides since then, but poverty and misery are still with us. The gap between what we have and what we want does not seem to have narrowed appreciably. The interests in near-death experiences and in angels are, I believe, surface eddies that indicate powerful currents of feeling under the surface. There is a strong sense of something important here.

When we concentrate the question of spirituality on the restricted concept of hell, that "something important" seems to gain force. For some, the whole notion of hell is absurd, no more than one of the fairy tales intended to terrify children into good behavior. For some, it is a constant fear; for others, an unthinkable contradiction of belief in a good and omnipotent God; and for still others, some a kind of myth with symbolic value but no basis in literal fact.

The most commonly reported near-death experiences (NDEs, for short) and angel stories tend to bypass the fear. They offer two assurances: that spirit is real and that it is, at least in the main, profoundly benevolent. In fact, some Christians have been alarmed at the beauty and gentleness of the "being of light" whom near-death experiencers so often describe. Where is the judgment? It sounds too much like one extreme of the human potential movement, like a claim that we are all intrinsically good and that evil is just some kind of misunderstanding.

If there is no judgment, what is the point of moral discipline? If I can make a comfortable living by cheating gullible old people out of their life savings, if I can use my sexuality manipulatively, if I can buy political power for my own ends, why shouldn't I? If there are no long-term consequences, surely the practical thing to do is to focus on the short-term ones. I might as well grab for all the gusto I can get, and then go out with a bang. The eighteenth-century pastor Jonathan Edwards offers a case in point. He was apparently a gentle and devout man who felt that his sermons were not really being heard. He called his flock to Christian living as persuasively as he could, but saw no change in their behavior. Finally, reluctantly, he preached on the terrors of hell, and it worked. People did begin examining their conduct and behaving more compassionately toward each other.

In a way, though, this misses the point. It argues simply that it can be a good thing to believe that there is a hell, and the usefulness of a belief is a separate issue from that of its truth. In a world far too complex for us to understand, we rely constantly on oversimplifications, on distortions that point us in the right direction. The notion of hell could be one of those oversimplifications, indefensible when examined closely, but in the main useful as a kind of moral compass. However, unless we realize that these statements *are* oversimplifications, they are likely to prove inadequate sooner or later. It sometimes seems as though every new discovery in the health field involves a discovery that things are just not that simple. I'm reminded of a headline from some years ago: "Schizophrenia Drug Called Major Advance: Potentially Fatal Side Effects Raise Concern." Life is full of side effects, and some of them can be fatal.

So the factual question remains, quite apart from the immediate and pragmatic one: is there really a hell? After death, will some of us find ourselves either temporarily or eternally in a state or place that merits that name?

I am not particularly interested in any of these as theoretical questions. In the following pages, there will be frequent references to contemporary events and literature. There will also be frequent references to Emanuel Swedenborg, an eighteenth-century gentleman who, over the last twenty-seven years of his life, claimed to have regular conscious experiences of a spiritual world, including experiences of hell. In scientific terms, these experiences would seem to defy replication. However, it was Swedenborg's assertion that we are unconscious residents of that spiritual world right now, that it is the world of our own deeper thoughts and intentions, and that what happens to us after death is that this inner, invisible world becomes visible.

In a sense, then, his descriptions of heaven and hell and especially of the intermediate state between them ("the world of spirits," which he sees as our present spiritual environment) can be tested against our own experience. His descriptions of that world are in some sense replicable. We may not have open experience of an alternative reality, but we can to some extent be aware of the workings of our minds. We may not have access to a hell that some enter after death, but we can look at the turmoil and pain of our own hearts and minds. This brings us down from the rarefied realms of theory to matters of immediate import.

In other words, the primary value of the descriptions for me is not as information about what is going to happen to us at some time in the future, but as images of what we are doing to ourselves and to each other inwardly here and now, highlighting the wellsprings of our inhumanity to each other. This eighteenth-century hell may throw some light on the turbulent world of the turn of the millennium.

There are several questions that need to be asked, simple on the surface perhaps, but challenging if we take them seriously, and the chapters that follow will center on these questions.

First, as a way of clearing the ground, I will look at issues of subjectivity and objectivity that necessarily arise in a discussion of "what we are doing to ourselves and each other inwardly." Chapter 2, laying further ground-work, treats of our nature as human beings. Chapters 3 through 6 deal with distinct aspects of hell—first, the na-ture of evil; then, its relationship to fear; then, the ques-tion of immortality; and, finally, the real possibility of our choosing hell. These will be followed by a personal re-construction, along Swedenborgian lines, of what differ-ent levels of hell might be like. The eighth chapter examines the language Scripture uses to describe hell; and the final chapter turns to the issue of theodicy, focusing on the function of freedom in reconciling the notion of hell with a belief in a wholly loving and omnipotent God.

In pursuing these basic themes, I have found myself touching on many others; and I am reminded that Swedenborg's view of hell is an inseparable component of a much larger picture and probably not readily compre-hensible outside that context. I have tried, however, to keep from straying too far from the subject of hell and to reconnect with it fairly promptly and clearly when I have digressed. There is an underlying hope that, if I push enough buttons, one of them may ring your bell.

The primary hope is that you may find thoughts in the following pages that help you see more clearly what lies at issue in our individual and societal lives. I was struck some years ago by the realization that, in the promise to Abram (Genesis 12:1–3), with such epic consequences, there is an imperative that is usually overlooked. It does not say, "You will be a blessing"; it says "*Be* a blessing." That, I firmly believe, is the only way to be blessed.

freedom & evil

WHat iN
tHe WORLÓ?

In the following pages, I will be recommending a particular view of our human situation. It is a view I have come to trust; but, before I present it, I want to acknowledge and even insist that it is by no means the only one possible. That is actually one of its intrinsic features. Let me offer a very simple image. Once when I was in high school, I was playing hide and seek with a neighbor's preschooler. At one point, he stood very still behind the horizontal branch of a fallen tree—I could see just about all of him except his eyes. It took a few moments for me to realize that he believed I could not see him because he could not see me. There was nothing wrong with his eyesight;

it was just that he could not yet realize that there were other perspectives than his own.

To use a somewhat subtler image, I have a four-piece puzzle that is a hologram of a starfish. You can see the whole starfish on each piece; and if you put them together appropriately, you see one starfish. As you move in relation to the picture, it "moves" on the surface of the hologram. This means that, if two viewers touch the end of one of the starfish arms as they see it, they will touch different places on the surface. Who is right? In one sense, they are both seeing the same thing, but no two agree as to exactly where it is.

I hope that what is quite obvious in regard to the physical world can be accepted as equally true of the mental world, namely, that things really, honestly do look different to different people. If people disagree with me, it is not necessarily because they are perverse. In fact, it can be genuinely hard to see things through someone else's eyes, to take seriously the fact that ours is not the only way of seeing things. It behooves us to listen to each other with a kind of noncompetitive spirit, then, without anxiety. Other perspectives may more properly complement than replace our own, giving us a multidimensional understanding rather than a plane one.

This is not an argument for radical subjectivity or "absolute relativism." I am not arguing that one view is as good as another or that there is no "reality" out there. I propose rather that the world is very real but far too complex for us to perceive with any completeness, so that even our most accurate perceptions are highly selective. My favorite illustration of this lies close at hand.

Choose some single letter near the center of this page, focus on it, and see how many words you can make out without shifting that central focus. The impression we have of seeing a page of clear print is an illusion, the product of our ability to scan. Only in the center of the retina are the photosensitive cells densely enough packed to enable us to perceive the detail we regard as normal. I am told that this area, the macula lutea, comprises *one forty-thousandth* of our total visual field. There is no question that the perception characteristic of that fraction is more adequate than the perception of the rest of the field; but still, which forty-thousandth will I choose to attend to?

How do we evaluate our selectivity? One of my mother's favorite stories was of the time her brother was unwillingly dragged to a concert of classical music. He wound up having a wonderful time because of the piccolo player. Uncle Jim spent the whole concert watching this very large man concentrate intently on playing this very tiny instrument. Acoustically, he must have heard the music. The sound waves struck his eardrums, the little bones rattled, the little hairs vibrated, the signals traveled along his auditory nerves; but his attention was elsewhere.

What he focused on was just as "real" as the music, but it would be hard to argue that it was as significant. Granted that the greatness of great music is impossible to quantify, it can be profoundly moving. The composer is trying to tell us something important, something that cannot be put into words. To focus on some little physical incongruity is like focusing on Abraham Lincoln's Adam's apple while he is delivering the Gettysburg

Address. Still, Uncle Jim enjoyed the evening when he might have made it miserable for himself and for the rest of the family.

Again, how do we evaluate our selectivity? One of the courses I took in my seminary days was a course in public speaking. Most of the time the teacher paid far less attention to what I was saying than to how I was saying it. That was what he was there for. I could have come up with the most brilliant insight of my life; but if my diction had been sloppy, if my dynamic range had been too limited, if my pace had been tediously steady, those aspects are what we would have talked about. As I write, I am trusting that this manuscript will be proof-read by someone who does not get distracted by the content, because it is all too easy to read what obviously *should* be there rather than what actually *is* there. By the same token, I hope that readers of the published work will not dismiss its thought because of transposed letters or errant punctuation. Swedenborg once noted in passing that we are capable of judging everything someone says on the basis of a single grammatical peculiarity.[1] I have heard an entire sermon discounted because of the use of a gender-exclusive pronoun.

All this seems fairly obvious, and what it indicates is that what is appropriate in one context may not be

---

1. *Arcana Coelestia* §241. As is customary in Swedenborgian studies, the numbers following titles refer to paragraph or section numbers, which are uniform in all editions, rather than to page numbers.

Except where noted, all quotations from Swedenborg's works are taken from the Standard Edition of the Works of Emanuel Swedenborg, listed in the bibliography at the back of the book. Wherever feasible, I will cite the work directly within the text, rather than in a footnote.

appropriate in another. It leaves us, though, with an urgent question: what do we mean by *appropriate*? Any dictionary will tell us that the word does not mean the same thing as *convenient* or *easy* or *profitable*, although human behavior does seem at times to reflect a belief that what is convenient or easy or profitable is self-evidently appropriate.

Tevye in *Fiddler on the Roof* acts out the issues we are dealing with. As his daughters depart further and further from tradition in their approaches to marriage, he finds ways to understand. On the one hand, there is the tradition, but on the other hand . . . . Finally, though, when a daughter decides to marry a Gentile, he reaches the boundary of his tolerance: "There is no other hand." As the script is written, this is not the story of a tolerant man finally cornered and defeated; it is the story of a rather weak man who finally finds his spine.

I do not believe, that is, that we are designed or intended to be moral crustaceans, fragile creatures protected from a hostile environment by a rigid shell of behavioral rules. I believe that we are designed and intended to be flexible and yielding in external matters and that we can do so only if we have an inner structure that is strong and supportive. There may be no "one-size-fits-all" criterion, but there is a definite constancy to the matter of "fitting." This, in turn, suggests that we need "the big picture," the picture that most adequately enables us to see how our view connects with other views.

We cannot stop there, though. That could leave us, as the old saying goes, loving the human race and hating people. Day after day, we find ourselves needing to focus on what is at hand. For a recent birthday, my wife gave me a telescope. It is powerful enough that it is just about impossible to locate any specific object at maximum magnification. There is a spotting scope, however, that offers a much wider field of vision, enabling the viewer to scan effectively and, so to speak, choose what to focus on. You can't see much detail in the spotting scope. By itself, it is not nearly as useful as a good pair of binoculars; but without it, the telescope is just about useless.

In presenting a particular view of our mental world, then, I will be trying to handle my own selectivity by alternately backing off and zooming in, trying not to get so lost in global considerations as to lose touch with immediate experience or so focused on minutiae as to lose perspective. Ideally, the two foci reinforce each other, the big view helping to define and delimit the importance of the details and the details confirming the relevance of the big view.

With this in mind, let me turn to (or at least toward) the topic of hell. Webster defines hell as "the place or state of punishment of the wicked after death: the abode of evil spirits." While I will later be questioning traditional notions of "punishment," I do see the definition as essentially valid. It says that we are dealing with matters of spirit, of value, and of consequence. That is, to talk about hell is to talk about something spiritual in the sense of nonmaterial ("after death"), something evil as to value, and something involving the consequences of evil.

It would be hard to pick three topics that are more important to our well-being, even to our survival, or three topics that better illustrate the lack of consensus of the world we live in. The notion that we are spiritual beings seems to some to be a delusive relic of medievalism, while to others, to be supremely important and virtually self-evident. As to the matter of evil, the news offers daily stories of human brutality that appall us on the one hand, and on the other hand evidence of vast differences in value systems, with some countries, for example, being accused of cultural imperialism because of their militant advocacy of "human rights." *We* may "hold these truths to be self-evident," but not everyone else does. In the matter of consequences, we are witnessing an ongoing tension between an assumption that technology can solve any problem it may create and a conviction that we are recklessly challenging inexorable laws of nature. We also find political theories of radical individual responsibility competing with theories of social determinism—very different notions of causality.

Turning first to the topic of evil, I may begin by observing that *evil* is not a popular word currently. It seems to have been banished from our workaday worlds, banished to nightmares on Elm Street and exorcists, reserved for figures of fiction. Certainly, it is a powerful word and should be used with caution. "Dysfunctional" or "counterproductive," yes, but "evil," no. Regardless of the fate of the word, it points toward things that we cannot ignore. Violence is not restricted to the silver screen and the domestic tube. If we look at the global situation, the inequities are little short of appalling, and we cannot help but be conscious of serious inequities within our own country. Immense energies are devoted to the elimination of various "isms"—sexism, racism, and the like—because, obviously, immense energies are being devoted to defending them. What we regard as evil and what we experience as its consequences can be quite literally matters of life and death.

As to spirit, if we multiply the notion of evil with the notion of immortality, the stakes are clearly raised. We can endure surprising amounts of pain or difficulty if there is real promise of better times ahead, of a light at the end of the tunnel. Athletes can push themselves to the limits of their tolerance of pain for the sake of the rewards they envision. The immediate result of many forms of surgery is not greater comfort but greater pain. It is only the long-term consequences that outweigh this, that make the immediate pain worth bearing.

Further, the matter of spirit is not just a matter of whether the consequences of evil extend beyond death. It involves also present sources of evil. If it is true that "out of the heart come evil intentions, murder, adultery, fornication, theft, false witness, slander" (Matthew 15:19), then that nonmaterial "heart" needs to be taken very seriously indeed.

As to causality, I opened this chapter by proposing not only that the world looks different from different perspectives but also that we might see these differences as complementary rather than competitive. This may be possible even for conflicting views of causality if they can be so related to each other that each has validity within a specific domain. Newtonian physics breaks down completely in the quantum realm, but it still works as well as ever in explaining the phenomena on which it was originally based. Or to use one of Swedenborg's illustrations (*Divine Love and Wisdom* §101), it may be that the earth is rotating and that the sun is relatively still, but for most of our daily transactions, it is much more efficient to talk and even to think in terms of sunrise and sunset. The moon as seen through my new telescope seems to travel across the viewing field. I see no particular point in insisting that it would be more accurate to say that the moon is relatively still and that the telescope is moving.

There is little point, that is, until we shift to a domain where the more limited perspective does not work. My friend and colleague Bob Kirven reminds me that he gets along just fine most of the time on the assumption that the world is flat, but he also knows quite well that on a larger scale, the curvature of the earth favors "great circle" routes, routes that by compass readings are not straight lines at all. The rotation of the earth makes a critical difference in the launching of space vehicles. No matter how efficient, how useful the parochial view is within its own domain, it is useless or even harmful beyond those limits.

This basic notion can be applied to our concepts of causality in the personal realm. Theories of social determinism and personal responsibility complement each other if the primary domain of the former is seen as the aggregate, the collective, while the primary domain of the latter as the individual. It is a familiar enough principle. My insurance company cannot predict with any precision when I will die, but it is prospering nicely because it knows quite accurately when "people like me" will die. Whether my own death comes tomorrow or when I am a hundred and twenty, it will have its place on the curve and will contribute to the precision of the actuarial table. In physics, the quantum events that are models of uncertainty add up to the ponderous reliabilities of matter.

Conversely, while the options open to me at any given time are limited by social determinants, those determinants do not tell me which option to choose any more than the predictability, the "certainty" of a stone limits the uncertainty of its electrons. This means also that my individual behavior does not precisely reflect the median of whatever class I am assigned to socially, ethnically, economically, linguistically, educationally, geographically, or in respect to age, gender, height, weight, amount or color of hair, or whatever.

If the class to which I belong cannot predict my behavior, that behavior may, however, be most intelligible only in the context of that class. Here, the analogy of language is useful. Every language has its own vocabulary and its own syntax, and acceptance of those structures is necessary for the communication of meaning. Similarly, every culture has a language of behavior, and acceptance of those structures is necessary for the communication of meaning. What is simple courtesy in one context may communicate condescension in another, coldness in a third, and intrusiveness in a fourth. What expresses simple affection in one context may communicate unwarranted familiarity in another or dangerous naivete in a third. The language, though, does not determine the message intended. If I know the behavioral language of my culture, it is still up to me to decide what I want to convey with it.

Further, I belong to many domains simultaneously. I am middle class, educated, male, senior, married, Christian, and so on. There is, in fact, no one else in my exact position in the fabric of society. As the son of well-educated parents who were hard pressed to make ends meet on the salary of a small-town minister, I grew up in "genteel poverty" without really realizing it. Our educational class and our economic class were poles apart. I did not know what the label "blue collar" meant, although any sociologist would have applied it to many of the families in our neighborhood.

If these classifications themselves can be concurrent, then social determinism and personal responsibility are concurrent as well, For the word *evil* to be at all useful, it must have some meaning that is reasonably constant throughout both domains. We cannot assign any specific temperature reading to the word *hot*—the temperature of a very hot day is the temperature of a very cold oven—but it points to the upper part of whatever scale is appropriate to the context in use. We will eventually need to proceed toward some kind of definition, to deal with the issue of value in Webster's definition.

The question of defining evil will have a chapter to itself. By way of preface, I would argue that what we call evil is significantly affected by what we call good and spend some time on that, recognizing that the definition of *good* has preoccupied philosophy since its inception. I am particularly (and perhaps predictably) attached to a definition offered by Swedenborg in *Divine Providence* §4.4. It is presented in impersonal terms—"A form is the more perfect as its constituent elements are distinguishably different and yet united"—but I find it widely applicable and especially persuasive in personal and interpersonal contexts. On the individual scale, it agrees with Ilya Prigogine's theory of dissipative structures, with his proposal that the entropy principle does not apply to organisms that respond to their environment because, when they face a challenge that is too complex for them to deal with, they are capable of developing new abilities. They can take into themselves some of the complexity they face and actually grow in responsiveness. On the collective level, it means that a community is more perfect as it nurtures individuals in their individuality *and* unites them in the service of common values. The community grows in responsiveness as it accepts and integrates individuals with different gifts. The basic principle suggests as well an intersection of social determinism and individual responsibility that is very much to the point.

This "good" is clearly dynamic rather than static. Individuals and their communities, or communities and their individuals, are interactive. For one thing, individuals are born, grow, change, and die. The actual constitution of any ongoing community is, therefore, constantly in the process of change. Then too, activity itself brings change. Some goals are actually attained, and new goals come to the fore. The victory of the Allies in World War II was decisive, but equally important were the postwar decisions that have left us with Germany and Japan as allies. It was the failure to make this shift of attitudes and goals at the close of World War I that sowed the seeds of World War II. Balkan history seems a particularly eloquent witness to the futility, the tragedy, of an inexorable determination to even the score, an inability to shift to a new agenda, as well as to the practical impossibility of simply choosing a status quo and maintaining it indefinitely.

This "good" is also elusive, in a sense subtle. On the global scale, how do differing cultures relate to each other? For all the anxiety about U. S. cultural hegemony, Germany and Japan are still different enough from America that we often have trouble understanding each other. When I ran into Russian resistance to "westernization" at a conference in 1992, it struck me forcibly that, even if our Russian hosts set out deliberately to imitate us, most of them would still be unmistakably Russian. It is hard enough to assimilate when you move to another country and live there for years. Korean students at our Swedenborgian seminary are acutely aware of the differences between first-generation, "1.5"-generation, and second-generation Korean-Americans. Koreans in Korea are undoubtedly being impacted by Americanization, but any sensitive visiting American will soon be aware of major differences in the cultural "language." The whole debate about ethnic identity and the "melting-pot" illustrates vividly the tension between individuality and unity.

As you may gather from the range of the examples above, part of the appeal to me of Swedenborg's definition of the good is the ease with which it transfers from one domain to another. A book I have found particularly enlightening is *The Evolving Self* by Robert Kegan.[2] In response to Carol Gilligan's critique of Kohlberg's theory of moral development,[3] Kegan proposes that we see our individual process as energized by

---

2. Robert Kegan, *The Evolving Self: Problem and Process in Human Development* (Cambridge, Mass.: Harvard University Press, 1982).

3. Carol Gilligan, *In a Different Voice: Psychological Theory and Women's Development* (Cambridge, Mass.: Harvard University Press, 1982).

the tension between our need for autonomy and our need for inclusion, which translate effortlessly—at least for me—into a need to be distinguishably different and a need to be united. The dynamic nature of this "good" stands out vividly in his description of our process as spiraling upward. Our appropriate efforts at self-assertion (to jump into the process arbitrarily at that point) lead eventually to a loneliness that impels us into closer relationships, which we find supportive until we begin to feel our individuality stifled and need to launch forth again.

This is, in Kegan's view, a spiral, not a circle. Each time we return to relationship, we have more to bring into it, and each time we launch forth, we do so with a stronger foundation of belonging. The gain is almost quantitatively perceptible in our unmistakable growth during childhood and adolescence, and more subtly true of our adult years.

The view not only translates readily to larger domains, but it also has necessary corollaries for them. In the immediate contexts of family and church, for example, it follows of necessity that the collective unit must be able to hold, to let go, and to be there—to support individuals when their primary need is for inclusion, to let go of them when their primary need is for autonomy, and to be there for them to come back to when the need for autonomy has run its course.[4]

It is worth noting that Swedenborg did not say, "A form is perfect when its constituents are distinguishably different and yet united." He said, "A form is *more* perfect *as* its constituents are distinguishably different and

4. Kegan, 158.

yet united." It is not a static picture of perfection attained but a fluid picture of perfection sought. The home changes when a child leaves or comes back. The church changes as individuals disengage or engage more intensively. The target keeps moving.

Further, the home and the church exist within larger contexts of community and have corresponding needs of privacy and of engagement, of times to close their doors and times to open them. In parenting, there can be an ongoing tension between family standards of behavior and the standards of the surrounding culture, the culture in which the children are learning to function. When our older daughter went to a private school, for example, it was a shock for her to discover that some of most decent and thoughtful students used language that appalled her and that some of the students whose language met family standards were people she would rather not associate with. Whatever the standards of the family, it seems that the peer pressure of early adolescence will challenge them. How do parents prepare children to negotiate this passage, to find the social acceptance that is so desperately important to them without compromising the integrity that is, in the long run, equally important? How open to the outside world should the family be? The personal, familial, and societal arenas are not at all discrete, and not necessarily in agreement.

The school is embedded in a still larger society, trying to do the ideal job of preparing its students to function in communities that are themselves far from ideal. I think particularly of teachers in the fields of the arts, teachers who are profoundly convinced of the worth of their subjects and acutely aware of their low value in the job market. Yet art, I would argue, is of immense importance to us. One of my recurrent fantasies is of creating a living environment in which there is no art whatever. The house would be the natural colors of whatever materials were used in its construction—no color schemes, no decorator fabrics, no pictures on the walls. Clothing would be chosen strictly for function, fit, and durability, with no dyes allowed. The radio and television would receive only factual information—no drama, no comedies, no music. The car would be as stripped down and utilitarian as possible, the office as bleak as the home. Everyone with a voice in the school budget would be required to spend a month in this environment before deciding what programs needed to be cut. I do feel crochety sometimes.

One clear implication of this is that the values of the embedding community are not beyond criticism. We need to proceed from domain to embedding domain, and it is becoming increasingly clear that we cannot stop short of the global. In *The Home Planet*, astronaut after astronaut speaks of the transformation of consciousness that comes from seeing our world as a planet, a single entity.[5] National boundaries do not exist. The atmosphere that our lives depend on pays no attention to them. The fallout from Chernobyl did not pause at the border to go through customs and immigration.

There was a delightful moment in a PBS special on snow geese some years ago. A family had followed them

---

5. Kevin W. Kelley, ed., *The Home Planet* (Reading. Mass.: Addison-Wesley Publishing Company, 1988).

north, camped out with them at their breeding grounds in northern Canada, and then followed them south during their fall migration. They had adopted and raised some orphaned goslings and had them in the car when they got to the U. S. border. When the customs official told them they could not bring them into the United States, they pointed up to the sky where hundreds of geese were "immigrating," just as their ancestors had been doing for centuries. For the record, the family let their geese out of the car, the geese followed the car across the border, and both nature and international law were satisfied.

The scale of domains from the individual to the global is basically a geographical one, two-dimensional. It is equally important to take time into account, given the frequency and familiarity of tensions between short-term and long-term considerations. Here again, it soon becomes evident that there is no one size that fits all. For a general rule, for example, I would propose that the long-term effects of parenting are primarily the effects of recurrent patterns of behavior and that traumatic moments are or seem particularly formative when they serve as summaries or images of those recurrent patterns. This means that the immediate demands of extraordinary circumstances may call for uncharacteristic actions that would have disastrous long-term consequences if they were repeated. If a child starts to dash out into the street, the use of force is appropriate even if a car is not coming. It is all very well to be suspicious of "Band-Aid" solutions, but I happen to have a Band-Aid on one finger as I type and am glad of it. Sometimes temporary measures are necessary as stopgaps. EMTs definitely have their place.

Clearly, though, if there is an eternal dimension, it needs to be taken with complete seriousness. This brings us to what is perhaps the subtlest tension between domains, the tension between the material and the immaterial. For me, strict materialism breaks down in the face of common experience. What we refer to as "immaterial" is not necessarily insubstantial. It resists change. Cars wear out long before driving habits do. Therapists of varying schools make their living helping people change deeply rooted patterns of thought and behavior that have become intolerable, and it is not easy work. It is impossible to argue that it is accomplished by the physical impact of the sound waves of the therapist's voice.

It can be difficult to change a long-held opinion and more difficult still to change or to resist a deeply ingrained attitude. The road to hell is paved less with good intentions, I suspect, than with unexamined ones, particularly deliberately unexamined ones. I am grateful to Rex Stout for the observation that "no man was ever taken to hell by a woman unless he already had a ticket in his pocket, or at least had been fooling around with the timetable."[6] *How* we do something affects others; *why* we do it affects us. Some of the effects on others may be immediate and obvious; the effects on ourselves are likely to be subtler, cumulative, and potent. I tend to look for evidence that supports my attitudes, so gradually those attitudes become more fixed. What attitudes am I reinforcing? Do I appreciate the myriad ways in

---

6. Rex Stout, *Some Buried Caesar* (New York: Bantam, 1982), 38.

which other people are both like me and different from me? Do I feel both akin to them and distinct from them? Can I appreciate and affirm their distinctiveness *and* keep them in the embrace of affection? These are questions central to my individual happiness and to our collective survival; and the languages of physics or neurology are wholly inadequate for discussion of them. At this point, then, we have touched on the spiritual element in Webster's definition.

The definition of *good* I am proposing is obviously not a list of virtues or a code of laws. It offers a basis for making judgments, that is, rather than a set of judgments pre-made. Any specific discipline is likely to have its code, its rules, which can be not only appropriate but necessary, given the particular purpose of the discipline. I have very fond high-school memories of Mr. Alkazin, the wood shop teacher who showed us how simple hand tools are to be used and cared for, and to Mr. Watson, who introduced us to the regularities and irregularities of French with irrepressible humor and inexhaustible patience. In each case, there were right ways and wrong ways, and there was little question as to which was which.

The complexities of human individuality and community are daunting enough, and the stakes high enough, to tempt one toward the same approach. Rule books offer a measure of security that has an undeniable appeal. So far, though, we do not seem to have managed to come up with a set of rules that is smart enough to outwit us. The Russian conference I mentioned earlier took place during the first flush of "perestroikal" optimism. One obviously prescient Russian sounded a cautionary note: "It seems as though every time we improve the system, the bad guys are first in line again."

The inflexibility of rules makes them particularly vulnerable to manipulation. I was once told by an employee of the FDA that that agency is rarely successful in prosecutions that depend on the minutiae of the rules such as placement of warnings or size of type. Most of their successes have rested on the demonstration of a clear intent to mislead when companies have tried to use the rules to their own advantage. No two situations are identical, which means that each one is to some extent a "special case." There is something to be said for principles that have wide applicability, that leave room for and in fact require judgment in their application.

But let me zoom in on the personal realm again, the realm where the question of hell is most immediately urgent. There is a phenomenon reported in many NDEs that humanizes the abstract principle of identity and inclusion in a way I find powerfully appealing. It is the phenomenon I mentioned in the preface as having raised the anxiety level of Christians who see it as undermining the notion of judgment. Individuals have described meeting a "being of light" who seems to understand them with perfect clarity and to accept them without reservation. All their faults are in plain view, all the things that they are ashamed of, *and* (not *but*) there is no trace whatever of condemnation or rejection. There is pure, loving understanding.[7]

---

7. The classic description may be found in Raymond A. Moody, Jr., *Life after Life: The Investigation of a Phenomenon—Survival of Bodily Death* (New York: Bantam, 1976), 58–64.

The unconditional acceptance is clearly a form of inclusion. The clarity of perception can be seen as a function of distinctiveness. There is no effort to blur distinctions, to fudge values, for the sake of inclusion. There is a little syllogism that may help. It is unfair to blame me for anything that is beyond my control. My past is beyond my control. Ergo . . . ergo, I am accountable essentially for the way I deal with the present effects of my past. It is appropriate to expect me to clean up the toothpaste, but not to expect me to put it back into the tube. "Charity," says Swedenborg in *The New Jerusalem and Its Heavenly Doctrine* §100, " is acting with prudence, to the end that good may result." Let me see what has happened just as clearly as I can and then respond just as constructively as I can. Let me see what has come apart, and then see whether it can be put back together. Alcoholics Anonymous very wisely requires its members to make amends for the harm their alcoholism has done to others, *where this is possible*. The qualification is important. If our goal is actually to assuage our own consciences, our focus is on our own benefit rather than on that of the people we have harmed, and there is a real risk of making matters worse instead of better.

Finally, the inclusion of identity and unity in "the good" opens the door for various approaches to any given problem. It supports working to change the system *and* working with individuals. Theologically, it supports spiritual *and* behavioral disciplines. There is no inherent conflict—in fact, no conflict whatever—between personal spiritual growth and a concern for social justice. They are indispensable to each other. Life can be full of vicious circles, and the image of the circle suggests that there may be more than one place where it is appropriate to intervene. There are people rushing to accident scenes to provide emergency medical attention, people working to design safer cars and safer roads, and people trying to discern and eliminate the causes of road rage in others and in themselves. We may be grateful that there are people who take to the streets and people who do not, that there are people who don't just sit there but do something—and people who in good Zen fashion don't just do something but sit there, trying to fathom the human soul. It would be a far less liveable world if everybody rushed to help, or if everybody just sat there.

WHO'S THERE?

Swedenborg's view of hell assumes certain characteristics of us as human beings and our human situation that have long been debated. While determinism asserts that everything we do is determined by past causes, Swedenborg assumes that we are basically free and purposeful moral agents. He further assumes that this purposefulness is central to our humanity, more significant than the strictly rational capacities that are sometimes identified as what distinguish us from animals. I would approach this subject by looking at two very common, basic words that we use as though we agreed on what they meant—specifically, *life* and *love*. If we really agreed about what these words mean, I suspect there would be much less conflict in our society.

As to *life*, the little Webster I have at hand is not much help:

> **life,** *līf, n.* state of living [defining it in terms of itself]: the sum of the activities of plants and animals [not what I am talking about]: conscious existence [suggestive, but consciousness itself is a mystery]: the period between birth and death [not, I believe, a primary meaning]: a series of experiences [ditto]: moral conduct [strongly context-dependent]: animation [= the presence of *anima*/soul or simply motion?]: a quickening principle [depends on the archaic meaning of "quick" as "living"]: a living being [defining it in terms of itself again]: living things [and again]: human affairs [not what I am talking about]: narrative of a life [ditto].

This is a relatively long entry for an abridged dictionary. It illustrates well the wide meaning range we are faced with and does well what a dictionary is supposed to do, namely, outline usage. It does not pretend to analyze or explain.

If we look at what is going on in our living bodies, things are not much clearer. We find both constructive and destructive processes constantly at work. Some cells are dividing, while some are dying. In the early phases of life, the constructive processes outstrip the destructive ones, and we grow in size and strength. There is a period of approximate stability and then a period when the destructive processes outstrip the constructive ones and our physical abilities wane. When we die, then, it seems not so much that the destructive processes have

accelerated—certainly not that they have just begun—
as that the constructive ones have slowed down and
stopped.

If we zoom out just a little, we find that this interaction of growth and decay is still very much in evidence. Virtually everything we eat was alive once and
has had to die in order to be "assimilated." Even vege-
tarians depend on the death of living plants. These living creatures give up their own identity, so to speak, so
that part at least of their substances can be reanimated;
and this is reanimated with our life, not with the life of
carrots and soybeans. This would seem to mean that,
whatever life is, it is not a substance or an inseparable attribute of particular substances. It is something that relates to particular substances and that relates variably.
The same substance, that is, can be part of a living
turnip on Monday and part of a living tight end on
Tuesday.

If we zoom out still further, we find ourselves to be
embodiments or instances of a pervasive ecological principle. The balance of nature depends on the interaction
of reproduction and death. When we have tried to alter
the balance for our own convenience, we have regularly
run into trouble. We eliminate predators, and deer multiply to the point that they devastate their own feeding
grounds and begin to die of starvation. We introduce
purple loosestrife to an environment where it has no
natural enemies, where nothing feeds on it, and it multi-
plies alarmingly. What would our own bodies be like if
the constructive processes were not counterbalanced?

Turning back to the matter of definition, perhaps
the most promising dictionary entry is "conscious

existence," especially if we allow for the possibility of some form of consciousness in plants.[1] Certainly if we look at "animal" forms, from the amoeba to the human, we attribute life when we see evidence of responsiveness, evidence that the organism is sensitive to relevant aspects of its environment. We infer this consciousness from the behavior of the organisms. The amoeba puts out pseudopods toward nourishment and retracts from toxins. We pull our chairs up to the table when we are hungry and push them back when we are full.

This brings us again face to face with the "unscientific" notion of purpose. I suspect that any doctor who has dealt extensively with terminally ill patients has room in his or her vocabulary for the phrase "the will to live," and, whatever that phrase may be referring to, recognizes that its presence or absence can have decisive effects. In fact, the language of purpose is so useful that it keeps cropping up in biology—birds sing *in order to* claim their territory, for example. A strictly deterministic account would be far clumsier: "Birds sing because birds that sing have had a higher survival rate because singing has the effect of establishing a territorial claim," or the like. In some instances, we can take shelter in words like *instinct* or *conditioned reflex*, but they rather beg the question. We label a reaction an instinct or a reflex when it is too quick for us to analyze: the more complex and slower the reaction, the more we are conscious of it and feel some control of it, and the harder it is to dismiss it in this fashion. We think in terms of intent, of

---

1. See, for example, Peter Tompkins, *The Secret Life of Plants* (New York: Harper and Row, 1973).

purpose. The will to live can be quite conscious and considered.

For Swedenborg, any effort to separate the topics of "life" and "purpose" is fruitless, since for him life *is* love, taking love in the broad sense of intentionality.[2] We are basically, fundamentally, goal-seeking creatures, and less complex forms of life simply show less complex and apparently less conscious forms of goal-seeking. In his definitive work, *The Treasures of Darkness: A History of Mesopotamian Religion*, Thorkild Jacobsen argues eloquently from his familiarity with early images of deity that we are dealing at first simply with "the will to be" in various natural phenomena—in grain or cattle or thunderstorms.[3] Only gradually, incrementally in fact, do these wills become represented in human forms, and only gradually do these humanized forms of natural wills interact in recognizably human ways, giving rise to myth. In every living thing (and in many things we would classify as non-living), the devout Mesopotamian saw a divine *purpose*, and that purpose was the essence of its life.

I find it impossible to dismiss such early views as merely superstitious. Perhaps it is science that is superstitious with its apparent belief that laws somehow make things happen. As far as I know, there is no measurable mass or energy to any law of physics, no material reality that could have measurable effects. Until Einstein posited the curvature of space, the action of gravity—action at a distance with no means of transmission of

---

2. Dictionary definitions of *love* focus mainly on concepts of warmth and affection. Swedenborg's highlighting of its motivational role is, I believe, important.

3. New Haven, Conn.: Yale University Press, 1980.

force—was theoretically impossible. It was the flight of the bumblebee on a cosmic scale. We might as well have posited "a mutual will to unite" as inherent in physical mass. At least it would represent an effort to explain what happens, rather than a pretense that there is no question to be asked.

In the first chapter, I argued that things looked different to different people and used the image of people standing in different places. The same basic image suggests that it makes a difference which way we are facing, what we are looking toward or for; and this is a matter of our purposes. Far more than we may want to admit, that is, we believe what we choose to believe. Given our genius for selectivity, it is hard to argue that the evidence compels us. I find Swedenborg saying that our choices about what we will believe are actually manifestations of our own will to be. I have an investment in my worldview. If I am a medical doctor, I *want* the medicines and procedures I recommend to be as effective as possible. If I am a physicist, I *want* reality to affirm my approach to it, to tell me that I am on the right track. I do not want to discover that I have spent years of study, years of professional advancement, traveling in the wrong direction. I will resist any suggestion that I have been wasting my life. If I am a theologian, I do not want to discover that matter is all there is.

The problem is complicated when we turn to what really matters most, to the values we assert in our dealings with each other. Here, we find our single selves inconsistent. On our good days, our more generous and considerate purposes seem inherently useful and attractive, while suspicion, resentment, and condemnation seem inherently repellent. On our bad days, things look very different. Generosity and trust seem weak and credulous, while suspicion, resentment, and condemnation feel quite realistic and promising.

Purposes, Swedenborg insists (for example, in *Divine Providence* §193), are what not only color but actually generate thoughts; and unless we are truly more imporant than anything else in the world, our strivings for supreme self-importance cannot generate anything other than distorted thoughts. We will see attractiveness in people who gratify us and ugliness in people who thwart us. We will see whatever we want as delightful and whatever we do not want as repellent. Helen Keller found words for this relationship between feelings and perceptions, stressing the affirmative side of it:

> As selfishness and complaint pervert and cloud the mind, so love with its joy clears and sharpens the vision. It gives the delicacy of perception to see wonders in what before seemed dull and trivial. It replenishes the springs of inspiration, and its joy sends a new river of lifelike blood through the matter-clogged faculties.[4]

She is here echoing Swedenborg, who spoke of a hierarchy of four fundamental loves—love of the Lord, of the neighbor, of the world, and of self. To start at the bottom of this series, all our concerns for what others think of us and for what we think of ourselves, all our needs

---

4. Helen Keller, *The Open Door* (Garden City, N.Y.: Doubleday & Company, 1937), 35.

for approval and respect, he gathers together in a category labeled "self-love" or "love of self," depending on what translation you pick up. That is Helen Keller's "selfishness and complaint." All our concerns for cars and clothes and cosmetics and CDs Swedenborg gathers together in a category labeled "love of the world." He can speak of our being "in" such loves, or of those loves "ruling" in us,[5] in which case our faculties become matter-clogged. We can get so wrapped up in ourselves or in our possessions that we are effectively blind and deaf to anything less obvious, anything that runs counter to those "loves," as he notes in *Arcana Coelestia* §7490, in just one example out of many.

We can get involved in something so thoroughly that it becomes our whole universe. It may be something as elegant as classical music or as primal as boxing, as popular as hard rock or as esoteric as the Sumerian verb. It may be a just cause or an ethnic group or a hobby. *What* it is does not seem to matter all that much. What matters is that we can lose all sense of proportion. I'm grateful to Professor Thomas Lambdin for one little incident along these lines. He was arguing strenuously a fairly obscure point of Hebrew syntax, and said, "Now many people . . . ," and then he paused. "No, that's not true," he said. "Not many people actually care." He was blessed with the ability to step outside the field to which he himself had devoted signal intelligence and immense energy and to see it in perspective.

Let there be no mistake, though. Swedenborg did

---

5. "Being in such loves" is, by far, the more frequently used. This expression and that of being "ruled" by such loves occur almost side by side in *Arcana Coelestia* §7367 and §7369.

not see these lower loves as evil in and of themselves. He was no ascetic. If we don't take care of ourselves, he says, we cannot be of any use to anyone else, he states in *The New Jerusalem and Its Heavenly Doctrine* §§97–99. Further, there is a definite place for recreation. Swedenborg's heaven is a realm of delight, and if we devote ourselves to a life of renunciation of delight, we "get ourselves a gloomy kind of life which is incapable of accepting heavenly joy" (*Heaven and Hell* §528). Food should not be our constant and overriding concern, but no one would deny that we need it in order to stay alive and active. Pleasure is a tyrannical master, but the prospect of a life without it is fearsome.

So much for the lower loves—what about the higher ones? In Swedenborg's language (obviously dependent on Scripture), the two primary higher loves are love of the Lord and love for the neighbor. Let's start with the second, since the neighbor is likely to be a more evident factor in our lives than the Lord. Why is solitary confinement regarded as such a severe form of punishment? What's wrong with being alone? Sometimes we really need some time to ourselves. But the fact seems to be that, in some very subtle and profound ways, we need human contact. Helen Keller wrote movingly about this:

> Sometimes, it is true, a sense of isolation enfolds me like a cold mist as I sit alone and wait at life's shut gate. Beyond there is light, and music, and sweet companionship, but I may not enter. Fate, silent, pitiless, bars the way. Fain would I question his imperious decree; for my heart is still undisciplined

and passionate; but my tongue will not utter the bitter, futile words that rise to my lips, and they fall back into my heart like unshed tears. Silence sits immense upon my soul. Then comes hope with a smile and whispers, "There is joy in self-forgetful-ness." So I try to make the light in others' eyes my sun, the music in others' ears my symphony, the smile on others' lips my happiness.[6]

Etymologically, *loneliness* and *desolation* are first cousins. What meaning would my life have if I were the only person on earth? Without input from other human minds, what would prevent mine from circling endlessly around itself? Absolute isolation and humanness are, I believe, mutually exclusive, and Helen Keller is obviously right in feeling the coldness of a sense of isolation and in turning to "others' eyes, others' ears, others' lips" to break out of the cycle of self-pity and depression. Her description gives a very personal flavor to Kegan's recognition of our need for inclusion.

She is saying more than that, however. She is saying that we are capable of self-forgetfulness. We can become so absorbed in a scene, a task, or another person that we are totally inattentive to what we may look like or sound like, totally oblivious to what's in it for us. An inspiring speaker, or the music that we particularly love, a task that demands our total concentration, or a child's joy or pain—any one of a number of things can open the way for this kind of consciousness.

Further, her point is not simply that we are capable

---

6. *The Open Door*, 51.

of self-forgetfulness but that self-forgetfulness is a locus of joy. It seems remarkable, on reflection, that the word *self-consciousness* so persuasively connotes discomfort. It calls up memories of times when we felt as though everyone was looking at us and seeing something they did not like. It suggests tension, anxiety, defensiveness. I wonder at times how many of our frustrations and disappointments come from striving for something that may not even exist—self-conscious happiness.

We may also be trying to *be* something that does not exist, namely, self-sufficient individuals. Physically, of course, I require constant nourishment. I seem not to be a delimited aggregation of matter, but a form through which matter moves or flows. Isolation from that flow would lead directly to death. Mentally, discerning which of my thoughts are mine, are original, and which are derived from others is a hopeless task. All of them seem to be both. I got this or that idea from Swedenborg, but no one else gets it in precisely the same way. In the realm of emotions, I would insist that, in a way, there is no such thing as "love"—there is only "love of." The first "not good" in the Bible is the divine statement that "It is not good that the man should be alone" (Genesis 2:18), a statement made even before the serpent comes on the scene. Whatever that statement may have meant in the days when myth was the language of serious thought, it has survived the millennia with impressive cogency.

But what of love of the Lord? Here I would turn to a Russian named Mikhail Kazachkov, a theoretical physicist who spent some thirteen years in a Siberian gulag. Trying to understand how his beloved country could have become so brutal to him and to itself, he came up with this answer:

> . . . a zero relationship to God. In the West, even if you are not a believer, the culture is so permeated with religious notions you are inevitably exposed to them. They form part of your personality. And whether you are prepared to agree or not, the notion of God is at the very center of your soul. Well, post-Communist Russia has a black hole in the middle of its soul. Every attempt to introduce democracy, market economy, decency, social fairness—anything which we hold dear, is sucked into that black hole.[7]

He was profoundly, passionately convinced of the need for an ontological foundation for human decency, for definitions of "the good" that rested on some reality rather than on the decisions of the state. There is something alarmingly wrong when the state can publish a paper called *Pravda,* "Truth," and actually believe that its contents are true simply and solely because it has published them. At its most fundamental, its most essential, and its most urgent, I would suggest that love of the Lord is a sense of being drawn toward a beauty of human goodness that does not originate in ourselves, that is a given, transcendent, and unchangeable part of the essence of reality itself.

---

7. Mikhail Kazachkov, "What Ever Happened to the Evil Empire?," unpublished talk given at a conference on Russian spirituality, sponsored by the Transnational Institute, held at Dartmouth College, 1992, pp. 11–12.

If this is so, then it is not only *Pravda* that should raise caution flags for us. We should be wary of any claim that things are true because they are "in the book," whether that book be the sayings of Chairman Mao or the Bible, *Mein Kampf* or the Qur'an. As a believer in a particular revelation, it is important that I realize that things are not true because they have been revealed; rather, they have been revealed because they are true. It is reality that has the last word, not a text about reality. Discovering and publishing the laws of physics does not make them true or effective, and disclosing spiritual laws does not bring them into being.

It is probably possible to start from this attraction toward a transcendent beauty of human goodness, especially if that beauty is seen in interpersonal rather than solely personal terms, and build a theology that has room for the rich variety of religions our world and its history display, but this is not the place for such a major enterprise. Paul Knitter presses in this direction in his effort to start with *praxis*, with common ethical concerns, rather than with axioms.[8] My own preference would be to move from this behavioral focus toward attention to character, rather along the lines drawn by Richard Hays' recent book on New Testament ethics, with the general effect not of proving the existence of a personal deity but of urging the essential sanity of this kind of belief.[9] But then, of course, I believe that our

8. Paul F. Knitter, "Toward a Liberation Theology of Religions," in *The Myth of Christian Uniqueness: Toward a Pluralistic Theology of Religions*, ed. by John Hick and Paul F. Knitter (Maryknoll, N.Y.: Orbis Books, 1987).

9. Richard B. Hays, *The Moral Vision of the New Testament: A Contemporary Introduction to New Testament Ethics* (New York: Harper Collins, 1997).

purposes generate our beliefs, that, especially in matters of value, we wind up believing what we want to believe.

Turning back to the higher loves, to the exent that we are absorbed in our awareness of others and are drawn to that kind of beauty—are "in love to the Lord and love for the neighbor"—we are not driven by fear of what others will think of us or do to us or by fear of what we will think of ourselves. This means (and this is absolutely critical) that we are now actually *more* likely to behave thoughtfully, because our perceptions are not clouded by those fears. Our self-concern does not fill the screen of our consciousness. We are actually able to focus on the other. We are also more likely to see the world as on our side, and perhaps paradoxically more likely to accept our own value and to be wise in our care for ourselves.

To the extent that we are inspired by a sense of a transcendent source of beauty, by a kind of awareness that the beauty of human goodness is not our invention but is intrinsic to reality, we are not driven at all, but are drawn. Swedenborg is particularly fond of the image of springtime to convey the way the growth of love brings everything in us to life; and we can surely hear in this fondness echoes of a lifetime's experience with long, dark Swedish winters, with every springtime a new miracle. This is just one example of the way in which his spirituality is earthly rather than otherworldly. It prompts an engagement with the world around us rather than a withdrawal from it. Our own bodies are instruments rather than prisons of our souls.

What is happening is that, although the lower loves deny the higher, the higher loves affirm the lower ones.

The higher loves then tend to amplify life, to include, while the lower ones tend to diminish it, to exclude. Self-glorification actually diminishes us. Care for each other enlarges us. Self-centeredness divides us against ourselves, puts us at war with ourselves, and we are the casualties of that war. If we limit our vision to our possessions, we diminish not only our world but ourselves. If we glimpse the beauty of the transcendent, everything comes to life, around us as well as within us.

The question is not simply what we care about, but what we care about *most*. "Status and wealth," wrote Swedenborg in *Divine Providence* §217, "are either blessings or curses." They are curses for people who regard them as ends in themselves but blessings to those who regard them as means to a useful life. There was a story circulating a decade or so ago about a young man who went into the world of finance with the resolve to make enough money to retire and do what he really wanted to do with his life, namely, be an artist. His friends, so the story went, thought this was a wonderful idea.

He apparently did very well, and one day announced that he had reached his goal and would be retiring and moving upcountry to start his real life as an artist. His friends now thought he was out of his mind to quit just when everything was going so well. They could not really see beyond the boundaries of their own preoccupations. Their purposes defined their vision.

There are cognitive consequences to self-absorption as well. When the something we get into is our own ego or some extension of it—some standard of living, some group, some standing in the community, some political party, some church—then we are partially blinded, and what we are blinded to is really what matters most. We are blinded to the fabric of mutual understanding and affection that being human is all about. There is such a weight of common sense behind truly humane values that an exhausting amount of mental effort is necessary to justify ignoring them. We have to distort what others are saying, belittle their intelligence, impugn their intentions, and basically construct an illusory world in which we are always right.

Robert Preus describes the attitude of orthodox Lutheran theologians in the centuries just following the Reformation:

> That their zeal for the truth might have appeared at times to be inflexible and extreme, at least to our calm and cautious age of theologians, that their intense loyalty to Christ and His Word might result in forgetfulness of even the closest human ties are hardly faults to be despised. . . . Particularly annoying to us today was the general practice among theologians of pressing the arguments of their adversaries to their logical but absurd conclusions. . . . It was as if neither party really listened to the other side.[10]

Or yet again, as my dear friend and colleague Bob Kirven once remarked, "Some of the most terrifying people I know are the ones who know God's will."

---

10. Robert D. Preus, *A Study of Theological Prolegomena*, vol. 1 of *The Theology of Post-Reformation Lutheranism* (St. Louis, Mo.: Concordia Publishing House, 1970), 29, 33.

The sense of being in possession of absolute divine truth must be immensely reassuring to anyone who has known the depths of insecurity, but it comes at the high price of inflexible resistance to doubt. Swedenborg was no stranger to doubt, and in fact saw it as a necessity for a healthy faith, as this excerpt from *Arcana Coelestia* §7298.2 indicates:

> No one should be instantly persuaded about the truth—that is, the truth should not be instantly so confirmed that there is no doubt left. The reason is that truth inculcated in this way is "second-hand" truth [*verum persuasivum*]—it has no stretch and no give. In the other life, this kind of truth is portrayed as hard, impervious to the good that would make it adaptable.

"The good that would make it adaptable" is essentially the affection for other human beings that inclines us to try to understand where they are coming from, that prevents us from dismissing their thoughts as simply wrong because they challenge our own. It is the attitude that profoundly does *not* want the other to be wrong, to be the enemy, not out of fear for our own safety but for grief at the destruction of a treasured relationship. It trusts that there is good in the other, so that there is no need to insist on being in control. It engenders the realism that genuinely admits the existence of a world outside the self, of people, people of real value, other than the self.

We are particularly vulnerable to rigidity when we identify so strongly with a group or a cause that we can believe we are acting in its defense rather than in our own. After all, we are not defending ourselves, we are defending the church, the truth. Read Eric Hoffer's *The True Believer*.[11] The syndrome is accurately characterized in a *New York Times* article about the effects of polarization in regard to the abortion issue: ". . . a political battle so passionate and divisive that warriors on both sides feel that all is fair, that no weapon is out of bounds, and that any admission of weakness could give the enemy an opportunity for total conquest." The article refers to "a new 'ethics of advocacy,' modeled after the combative behavior of lawyers in a courtroom, in which the quality of facts takes a back seat to the deftness of their manipulation."[12] I am puzzled only by the notion that this ethics of advocacy is new. More probably, it's old as hell.

That eminent postmodernist Francis Bacon complained, "The Idols of the Theatre have got into the human Mind from the different Tenets of Philosophers and the perverted Laws of Demonstration. All Philosophies hitherto have been so many Stage Plays, having shewn nothing but fictitious and theatrical worlds."[13] At this point, it seems to me that strict determinism breaks down completely. If everything happens inevitably as a result of previous events, where does error creep in? What causes *it*? Surely the existence of an omnipotent God ought to have inevitable effects on our

---

11. Eric Hoffer, *The True Believer: Thoughts on the Nature of Mass Movements* (New York: Harper and Row, 1966).

12. Frank Bruni, "The Partial-Truth Abortion Fight," *The New York Times*, 3 April 1997, "The Week in Review" section.

13. *Novum Organum Scietarum*, section 2, aphorism 7.

consciousness. But then, if there is no such being, what could cause us to invent such an unreality? Or could there by any chance be an omnipotent God who wills our freedom, an omniscient God who intends that we should make up our own minds, an omnipresent God who intentionally leaves room for our individuality? Could there be a divine uncertainty principle?

It is in some respects not an easy notion to swallow. We are utterly dwarfed by the vastness of our solar system, which is dwarfed by its galaxy, which is dwarfed by the observable universe. I see no way to avoid the conclusion of Yitzhak Bentov that an expanding universe sets an absolute boundary to our own observations.[14] Take a star ten light years away from us and a star twenty light years away from us. Given a constant rate of expansion, the first is moving away from us at a given rate, and the second is moving away from the first at the same given rate, moving away from us, then, twice as fast as the nearer one. At some point, that relative speed will reach the speed of light, so the light from any galaxies beyond that point will never reach us. The notion that there is a God who created all this (or in Swedenborgian terms is constantly creating all this), who is omnipresent and omniscient, is in and of itself staggering. When we try to put it together with the notion that this deity cares about us as individuals to the point of hearing our individual prayers, the difficulties are very real.

Or are they? In a truly postmodern conceptual framework, things are different. We might rather start

14. Yitzhak Bentov, *Stalking the Wild Pendulum* (New York: Bantam, 1979), 172–173.

with the difficulty of believing that our own little minds can conceive of such vastness. We have never experienced a single light-year, we have barely begun to travel beyond the intimate limits of our own planet's atmosphere, we are incredibly tiny, transitory beings. It is the reach of our own tiny minds that dwarfs us.

How do we explain that reach? Is it really a kind of illusion caused by the random collisions of unimaginable numbers of mindless particles? If I can manage to believe (which I cannot) that the entire cosmos, including the sum of all human thought, came into being as a result of such collisions, can I believe that it is also maintained by sheer chance? What are the odds that one pair of particles will misbehave and that the whole fabric will start to unravel? Those odds must be increasing by the size of the universe every instant.

Entia non multiplicanda sunt praeter necessitatem is the "razor" attributed to Ockham—don't make things more complicated than you have to. Whatever the explanatory power of determinism in explaining many physical events, it immensely complicates any explanation of the emergence of intelligence, and it breaks down completely when it comes to describing interpersonal events, let alone explaining them. I would urge that the hypothesis of purpose—in fact, of love—as intrinsic to the universe is a hypothesis that works. Life emerged in the course of time because it was inherent in the process from the start. Intelligence emerged in the course of time because it is inherent in love.

In fact, I doubt that even the most resolutely deterministic scientists have managed to live up (or down?) to their theories. I suspect that they see themselves as purposeful beings and feel frustration when their purposes are thwarted. I suspect that they treat their students as responsible agents, holding them accountable as though they were in control of their choices. As I have already suggested, I suspect that they regard determinism as a conclusion they have reached by the free exercise of their minds and believe that others can choose to agree with them. The obvious consequence of strict determinism would be completely obsessive-compulsive behavior, and this is scientifically classified as a mental illness.

Let me conclude this chapter, then, by connecting it with the main theme of the book. The widest context of the Swedenborgian hell, the ultimate presupposition behind it, is a God of infinite love and wisdom. This is the source of the order in the cosmos, an order which finds its most complete expression in beings capable of appreciating it and in some measure emulating it. The abilities to love and to discern interact in those beings (us) in such a way that we have the recognizable ability to make significant choices, including choices between competing loves and competing understandings of our world and of each other. To the extent that we accept and affirm this deep nature of reality, reality is necessarily on our side. We are accepted and affirmed. To the extent that we set ourselves against this deep nature of reality, we feel ourselves opposed at every turn.

Hell, then, is by no means incompatible with the existence of a loving and omnipotent God. It is a necessary consequence of the existence of such a God unless our own destinies are determined by that omnipotence. If they are so determined, then perhaps our doubts of

God's love are deepened rather than relieved regardless of our conclusions about the reality of hell. Am I to understand God's omnipotence to mean that we have no power, that I do not have the power to write, or you the power to read? Or for that matter, what kind of God would let us suffer so much if we are all going to wind up in heaven eventually in any case? What purpose has the suffering served? Has it done anything more than foster the illusion that our choices make a difference? If all roads lead to the same destination, what is the point of the long, tortuous, rocky ones?

Perhaps the central message of the book of Job is not so much the answer that comes at its close as it is the intensity of Job's argument with his creator. Like the bush in the wilderness of Midian, Job burns and burns, *and is not consumed.* I think also of Jonah sweltering in the sun and saying to God, "I do well to be angry, even to the point of death" (Jonah 4:9). I think primarily, though, of the crucifixion of the one who was Immanuel, God with us, as the ultimate image of divine refusal to override human rejection—even to the point of death. This may may tell us that the problem of theodicy is not one of degree but of kind.

WHat's WRONG?

Against this background, let us turn to the question of evil. Evil is central to any definition of hell, but I doubt that any two people would agree precisely on what it is. William Blake leveled scathing criticisms against the church of his time for demonizing energy and creativity and making a virtue out of self-righteousness. Some cultures regard as evil certain freedoms for women, while others regard as evil the denial of those freedoms. In a sense, simply by doing something we assert that the something is "good" or is at least the best we can manage under the circumstances. Some theologies regard this world as evil, while to others, "all nature sings, and 'round [us] rings the music of the spheres."

About forty years ago, school children had "duck-

and-cover" drills—what to do in case of a nuclear attack. Any child with half a brain knew perfectly well that a wooden desk would give about as much protection as a wet paper bag. Somewhere in the back of a lot of young minds, and in the front of some, was a sense that they would never live to see adulthood. Anyone who predicted that we would arrive at the year 2000 without one instance of nuclear war would have been labeled a dreamer, a hopeless optimist. Here we are. *Something* seems to have gone right.

For some reason, we seem to think that realism means facing how rotten everything is. C. S. Lewis called attention to this in *The Screwtape Letters*. Lewis' Screwtape is well up—or perhaps better, down—in the "lowerarchy" of hell, and Wormwood is a kind of devil-in-training assigned to secure the soul of one particular individual. The letters are instructions from the teacher to the intern, and at one point Screwtape urges Wormwood to take advantage of our human susceptibility to pessimism. One of hell's great successes, he says, is that people now seem to believe that everything ugly is real and everything beautiful is only subjective:

> The creatures are always accusing one another of wanting "to eat the cake and have it"; but thanks to our labours they are more often in the predicament of paying for the cake and not eating it.[1]

Read the front pages of any newspaper, and it will seem as though every other person is a criminal or a vic-

1. C. S. Lewis, *The Screwtape Letters* (New York: MacMillan, 1954), 153–154.

tim. Read the obituaries, and it will seem that, for every one person who makes the front pages, there are hundreds who have lived quiet, decent, constructive lives. In the early days of *glasnost*, the Russian satirist Mikhail Zhvanetsky sounded a warning to his fellow citizens. He described an American store:

> There's nothing special there, just everything. . . . That's half of it. And half of it is what we don't know, haven't seen or heard. . . . Someone is doing it all. Someone is working. . . . If we here, through many centuries of struggle, through deprivation and disasters, earned the sacred right to do absolutely nothing for 100 rubles a month, over there, on the other hand, to stand in place, you have to run.[2]

Why mention this? I'm going to be talking about hell, about evil, for most of this book, and I want to set the discussion in context. It's much too easy to say that evil is real and that good is an illusion, but that doesn't do much more than express the way we may feel about things. There are thoughtful and loving people who believe that we are nothing but evil, who regard any claim of goodness as blasphemous. There are thoughtful and loving people who take the opposite tack, who, like Christian Scientists, believe that evil is nothing but an illusion. Norman Vincent Peale argued for the power of positive thinking, and millions of people discovered that, for them, it worked. I'd rather assume that good and evil

---

2. From the *New York Times*, n.d., "Week in Review" section.

are equally real facts of life, that some really good and some really bad things do happen. I would also insist on distinguishing what we are from what we claim to be, that is, between goodness and any claim of goodness. I suspect that the extremes of a doctrine of total depravity and a doctrine of positive thinking work primarily as antidotes to an excess of the opposite and that each is therefore also capable of exacerbating an existing condition.

I believe that we ourselves can *be*, from time to time and even predominantly, "really good" or "really bad." There may not be any examples of absolute perfection, but there are people who are consistently perceptive and thoughtful, who seem to enjoy looking for ways to make things a little better for those around them. Some televangelists may have given the clergy a bad name, but a recent survey discloses that the vast majority of ordinary clergy are much better at giving than at asking others to give.

There is a huge difference between such people and the ones M. Scott Peck describes in *The People of the Lie*.[3] The examples he gives of ordinary evil people are, to me, truly frightening. These are not criminals in the legal sense. They are not wearing hockey masks or wielding chain saws. They may not even be breaking traffic laws. These are parents or spouses who seem simply not to care about anyone but themselves and who see themselves as perfectly okay. Nothing gets through to them. They construct their own definitions of right-

3. M. Scott Peck, *People of the Lie: The Hope for Healing Human Evil* (New York: Touchstone, 1983).

eousness and live wholly within the impregnable walls of those definitions. Their impact on the lives of people close to them is disastrous.

Let me pause a moment to emphasize that, while I will be zooming in and out, my primary focus in the book will be on our treatment of each other, on interpersonal relations, with no great gulf between that and how we treat ourselves, on what we might call *intra*personal relations. This, I believe, is the area that matters most to most of us. This is where we feel our deepest joys and pains. Ask the elderly what they would do differently with their lives if they had them to live over again, and this is the area that consistently comes to the fore. "I would spend more time with my family." Someone can be a very good scientist or mechanic or cook or golfer and not be a very good person, and there is a great deal of evidence that this latter goodness is ultimately more important to us than the former ones. However skilled or successful we may be professionally, if we are trapped in the kind of self-absorption Peck describes, life is grim both for us and for those around us.

It is important at this point not to oversimplify the contrast. If, as certainly seems to be the case, the good folk are not perfect, the evil ones are not absolutely evil.[4] There are instances of people who have really turned their lives around. Sometimes it has taken a tragedy of major proportions; sometimes it seems as though individuals can simply wake up to the harm they

---

4. According to Swedenborg, every human being has an inner angelic nature that opting for evil does not destroy but closes off. See, for example, *Arcana Coelestia* §7442:2 and 9256:2; and *Divine Providence* §139.

are doing. *Amazing Grace* was written by a man who had captained a ship in the slave trade, surely one of the most inhuman, evil practices imaginable. When he wrote, "I once was lost, but now am found, was blind, but now I see," he meant it passionately. It is hard to imagine the cost of that change, the pain of that awakening. It is surely significant that the pain did not destroy him. He meant "how sweet the sound" passionately, too.

We evidently have some awareness not only that we can *be* good or bad, but that we can *choose* to be good or bad. When we find people who feel that they have no such choice, we start talking about obsession and compulsion, about psychosis. The insanity defense in criminal law rests on the assumption that we can normally tell good from bad, murder and rape and sadism from thoughtfulness and faithfulness and honesty; and that, if we cannot, there is something seriously wrong with us.

So if simply labeling some people as good and others as evil is a dangerous oversimplification, it may be equally dangerous simply to say that somewhere down inside there is something good in everyone and blame destructive behavior entirely on circumstances. This, I would insist, is to apply to the individual realm what works only in the collective realm. It is, if you will, to regard electrons as rocks. In a more personal vein, to deny individual responsibility is essentially to deny human freedom. It makes robots of us *all*—not just of the oppressed, since the privileged must be equally creatures of their circumstances. Perhaps we should talk about people who are "gooding" and people who are "eviling," presuming that there are competing voices in all of us and that, while we may never entirely silence either, we may fairly consistently affirm either the good or the bad.

Of course, circumstances make a difference and must be taken into account. The principle expressed in Luke 12:48—requiring much of those to whom much has been given—makes all kinds of sense. It is all too easy to live wonderful lives in the "if only" world, to imagine what we would do if circumstances were different. One of my adolescent fantasies involved being married, finding a house that was so shabby we could afford it, and then transforming it into an attractive home. Some years later, while I was struggling with some particularly recalcitrant wallpaper on a hot, humid summer day, it dawned on me that this was my dream come true. It didn't feel at all like my fantasy, though; and that left me with an awareness that my fantasies about what it would be like to be rich or famous or powerful were surely just as unrealistic.

One other experience comes to mind. It happened when I was in graduate school, working the long and intellectually strenuous hours of the doctoral candidate. A friend and I decided to splurge and go to a football game and to have some friends in for beer and munchies after the game. When the time came to leave for the stadium, I couldn't find my ticket. Eventually, I sent my friend off and settled down to listen to the game on the radio. I was wallowing along in self-pity when it dawned on me that the only thing wrong with my situation was my standard of comparison. The reality was that I was taking the afternoon off from work and listening to a football game, expecting friends to drop in afterwards—

hardly the stuff of martyrdom. I'm still not sure why that worked, but it did. I had a thoroughly enjoyable, relaxing afternoon. When I found my ticket some months later, I felt like framing it as a reminder to focus on doing what can be done with the circumstances that actually exist rather than wasting time imagining how much better life would be "if only." When virtue is inevitable, relax and enjoy it.

Just how *much* difference do circumstances make? As the world shrinks, we discover that other cultures have values that seem strange to us, sometimes values that offend us. But surely it is not culture that decrees that cruelty and avarice and deceit are bad. Most of us sense, I believe, a difference between real good and real evil that we do not invent, however various the ways we find to express it. Strenuous as it may be, I would urge that we work hard to draw the line between universal moral values and behavioral relativism and not to allow either to encroach on the territory of the other. If we cannot afford the tyranny of moralism, neither can we afford the anarchy of moral oblivion.

Let me start toward a definition of evil by proposing that real evil must be what is really bad for us. This sounds so obvious as not to be saying anything at all, and it is intended only as a first step toward a definition. It is a definite step because it says that evil is not something that is simply against a set of arbitrary rules. To use a strictly physical analogy, stealing a cookie from the cookie jar is not bad for me in the same sense as drinking drain cleaner. If stealing the cookie is really evil, it must be because it does harm on some level, apparently on some level other than the physical. If it does no harm, what is wrong with it?

One dimension of that harm, perhaps even a principal one, is that it asserts a distortion. It is a behavioral claim that the cookie is mine, that I am entitled to it, or, more fundamentally, that my needs outweigh the needs of others simply because they are mine. To move from the trivial to the tragic, such attitudes as racial bigotry and homophobia demand a profound distortion of our perception of those who are hated. In the fragmentation of what was once Yugoslavia, we can see Serbs, Croats, and Muslims all engaged in demonizing each other. From the outside, at least, it looks like a deliberate refusal to admit the enemy's claim to human standing.

This is, of course, a prerequisite for effectiveness in war. If one is flooded with a sense of kinship with the creature in one's gunsight, it is hard to pull the trigger. Propaganda regularly dehumanizes the enemy. The Germans we fought in my childhood, in World War II, were not fathers of children or storekeepers or people who might live next door to us—they were Krauts, Nazis, without individuality. The dehumanizing is all the easier when there is a racial difference. The political cartoons of a war era use grotesque caricatures of such differences and infuse them with malice and bestiality. This was unnecessary in the Gulf War because it was fought at such long range, at least from our armchair perspective. We saw laser-guided bombs striking buildings with uncanny accuracy. We saw night skies filled with anti-aircraft fire with apparently total ineffectiveness. The impression was that the only times our soldiers saw Iraqi soldiers was when the latter surrendered.

It seemed like a war of our military machine against theirs, not a war of us-against-them in any personal sense.

I am not concerned at this point to demonstrate or even to claim that war itself is evil. I want simply to argue that there is something about evil that deliberately and systematically distorts perceptions, hoping it is clear than any such distortion lessens the likelihood that our decisions will be appropriate, that our actions will actually have the results we intend. If I am driving and misperceive the distance between my front bumper and the rear bumper of the car in front of me, actions intended to avoid a collision may cause one instead.

One element of a definition of evil, then, may be just that: evil distorts perceptions and divorces us from reality. To relate it to the definition of good in the first chapter, evil makes distinctions where they are inappropriate and ignores them where they are appropriate. The flourishing of postmodernism has been fertilized by the extent to which we live in worlds of our own, sometimes carrying this to the extreme of claiming that we actually create these individual worlds. As I have already suggested, it makes far more sense to me to claim that we build such worlds out of available material, that we do not so much create as select; and it also makes sense to me to believe that some of our constructions are more valid than others. Attitudes that promote illusory constructions should be no more welcome than scientific procedures that regularly yield distorted results.

Swedenborg, incidentally (but not coincidentally), agrees. He insists that we never attain pure truth, that our minds are capable only of comprehending appearances of truth, but that appearances can be more accurate or less so (see *Arcana Coelestia* §3207). I am grateful to Huston Smith for many things, among them his observation that just because you do not have 20/20 vision does not mean that you are blind.[5] Everyone with any degree of sight sees *something*. Trained observers see more than untrained ones. No one sees everything there is to be seen. At different times, I have walked through a particular stretch of Maine woodland with an artist and with a forester. The artist called my attention to colors I never would have noticed. The forester called my attention to signs of health and disease that I never would have noticed. Both, I am sure, could tell how their perceptiveness had developed with experience.

The experience of blind people who have recovered sight is striking. We so take for granted our ability to interpret the impulses that travel along our optic nerves that we have no idea how extraordinary that ability is. One newly sighted man spoke of knowing what a dog was sequentially. He had run his hands over dogs, and knew how head and back and legs and tail followed each other in tactile fashion. He found it almost impossible to relate that knowing to seeing a dog simultaneously, all at once. He knew from variations in volume how far away people were from him; he was unprepared for their instantaneous presence in his visual field, regardless of distance.[6]

---

5. Huston Smith, "Introduction," in George F. Dole, *A Thoughtful Soul: Reflections from Swedenborg* (West Chester, Penn.: Chrysalis Books, 1995), x.

6. Oliver Sacks, "To See and Not To See," *The New Yorker*, May 10, 1993: 59–73.

We, on the other hand, have learned to correlate size with distance. I was suspicious of Swedenborg's statement that we judge distance by intervening objects until I looked down from the upper observation deck of the tower in Toronto. I could have sworn that the lower deck was only a little above ground level. In fact, it was not much below the upper deck, but there was nothing between me, it, and the ground to "read." We acquire this skill in infancy, it seems, and then forget completely that we have learned it.

We did have to learn to see, however, and any teacher will testify that attitude is critical to learning. I suspect that the attitude most conducive to learning a subject is simply a fascination with the subject itself. In second place might be a realization that the subject is intrinsically necessary for some desired goal. In third place, we might find the attachment of some arbitrary reward, and in fourth place, the threat of punishment for failure.

I suspect also that teachers could, if pressed, also identify attitudes that militate against learning. I know of a child, for example, who in junior high was a valued member of a nationally ranked math team at the same time he was flunking math. Feelings of inadequacy, resentment of a teacher, resentment of a subject, general emotional turmoil—any or all of these may disable a perfectly capable intelligence.

It is when we turn to interpersonal and intrapersonal relations that this begins to touch us to the quick. We are beginning to identify and face some of the facts and effects of the physical abuse of children. We seem to be still in a kind of limbo when it comes to verbal abuse, to the effects on children of being told that they are stupid or worthless, that they are unwanted and unwelcome, that their parents' life would be better without them; but we are closer to facing such facts in regard to parenting than we are in regard to relationships between adults. That is, we have no compunctions whatever about restricting freedom of behavior, passing laws that forbid doing physical harm to each other. When it comes to our verbal behavior, on the other hand, we cite the principle of freedom of speech and give ourselves license to inflict all kinds of psychological and spiritual pain on each other.

As I was working on this chapter, a friend told me a story. He had worked as a teacher in a factory that had a high percentage of immigrant labor. The 550 employees included people who spoke fifty-three different languages, and part of his job was helping them with their English. At one point, he was trying to explain the word *hobble* and asked whether anyone there had ever had a broken leg. There was a space of silence, and then one woman from Viet Nam said, "I have a broken heart." Granted that what happened in Viet Nam was violently physical, this woman herself was not telling of having been physically hurt. In a sense, she was saying that she had *not* been hurt physically. She had been hurt more deeply, more seriously, more lastingly, by what she had seen and heard.

We do such things to each other on scales from the intimate to the global, and I would urge that they are not different qualitatively just because they are different in scale. "Whoever is faithful in a very little is faithful also in much, and whoever is dishonest in very little is dishonest also in much" (Luke 16:10). About twenty years ago, I was confronted by a very earnest young evangelical Christian who was convinced that Swedenborg was a spiritualist and that Swedenborgians were in danger of eternal damnation. I was not about to get into a proof-texting competition and could not find any way to defend my faith without at least seeming to impugn his, so we eventually parted company with a sense of stalemate. Reflecting on my discomfort afterwards, I was faced with the fact that my desire to get away from him was essentially a desire not to have him in my world. Turn up the volume of that desire enough, and you have the Holocaust and the mushroom cloud.

The closest I can come to defining the essence of evil is that real evil, whether grand or petty, is the ultimate zero sum game. That is, if every increase in my happiness (which we can and must extend to include "my party's" or "my team's" or "my church's") means a decrease in yours, if every increase in yours means a decrease in mine, no culture on earth can devise a way to satisfy us both. There is no way you can be different from me and united with me. Ultimately, I will your destruction. This may play itself out in any number of ways, some of which we will be looking at later. On the other hand, if I find delight in your happiness and you in mine, we can probably manage to find ourselves at home in almost any culture imaginable.

This may not be as easy as it sounds. Definitions of evil are obviously closely related to definitions of good, probably dependent on them, which brings us back yet again to the definition of good proposed in the past chapter, the simultaneous affirmation of values that are often in tension, namely, difference and unity. In human terms, this means individuals bringing their distinctive gifts into the service of the community, and the community treasuring both the gifts and their distinctiveness. Individualism and communalism, autonomy and interdependence, need not be in opposition, but they often are. While it may not hold up to close scrutiny, there is the appearance that American communities are threatened by an overemphasis on individualism, while the Soviet system sacrificed the individual to the collective, to the state. This contrast needs to be qualified by the observation that Americans can be hopelessly conformist and Russians radically individualistic. We seem to find it impossible to have more than two major political parties. I'm not sure that the Russians have brought it down to double digits. The side that is officially or culturally repressed may work all the more powerfully for being unseen. Still, on smaller scales, I suspect most people have experienced both tendencies, have felt their appeal and experienced their liabilities, and have found themselves torn between them. They may belong together, each supplying what the other cannot, but getting them together takes time and effort.

If the good is this complementary relationship, then one extreme of evil involves the effort to destroy unity; and one way of doing this is by maximizing difference, by demonizing the other. It may be hard to believe, but there have actually been supposedly Christian views of heaven that portrayed the blessed as entertained by watching the suffering of the wicked, especially of heretics. Isaac Watts said it with appalling clarity:

What bliss will fill the ransomed souls,
When they in heaven dwell,
To see the sinner as he rolls
In quenchless flames of hell.

This sounds terribly like adolescent fantasies of revenge, like an appeal to one of the ugliest aspects of human nature. One biblical text that comes to mind is Ezekiel 18:23: "Have I any pleasure in the death of the wicked, says the Lord God, and not rather that they should turn from their ways and live?" Then there is Paul's statement that "love does not rejoice in wrongdoing but rejoices in the truth" (1 Cor 13:6), and there is the pervasive theme of forgiveness, of love of one's enemies, in the Gospels.

In fact, in the zero-sum concept, the very heart of evil is delight in the suffering of others. This destroys the humanity of the individual who indulges in it, and it destroys human community. Good is not something cultures invent in order to survive. It enables cultures to survive because of its realism, because it faces the way things work whether we like it or not, whether we admit it or not. In a very real sense, then, good *is* the way things are. It *is* good that evil is self-defeating. Any other arrangement would be unthinkable. If evil worked, it wouldn't be bad.

Swedenborg expresses this theologically by saying that "The Lord rules the hells" (*Heaven and Hell* §536). The same principles hold in the company of the evil and in the company of the good. There is no way to beat the system. There is no way that brutality can bring about peace of mind or abiding community. No amount of deception or self-deception can make evil good. In fact, it takes a great deal of self-deception to convince ourselves that evil is good. Somehow or other, unfortunately, we can manage it if we try.

There is another aspect of this that is obvious once it is pointed out, namely, that as evil is inherently destructive, falsity itself is essentially impotent. The classic example of the shady character who tries to sell you the Brooklyn Bridge for ten dollars will do as a case in point. In order for a scam to be effective, it has to be plausible, it has to sound something like the truth. We do have a remarkable capacity for wishful thinking. Time after time, we read of people who have lost their life savings to "nice" people who promised miracles. But still, the nice man has to offer even our most wishful thinking *something* to work with. If he were to say, "I'll throw your money up into the air, and it will triple before it falls back," even the most gullible of us wouldn't bite. Hypocrisy, someone has said, is the tribute evil pays to good.

If one effect of evil is to distort perception, then, evil gravitates toward futility. The harder I try to make the world conform to my specifications, the more out of touch I become with what is actually happening, and the harder still I have to work. This is not to say that the good guys will always win, not at all. It is to say that a life of increasing self-absorption will become harder and harder to sustain mentally, while a life open to the reality of my fellow creatures will become increasingly easier. I find the Taoist image of sensing and cooperating with the currents of reality immensely sane.

There is an analogy or instance in the field of

ecology. We may and do for our own purposes misperceive or disregard the laws of ecology. They are complex
and gradual enough to offer us a great deal of wiggle
room. If we do actually distort these laws and act on our
distortions, however, the pressure builds. They continue
to work whether we acknowledge them or not. Eventually, the time comes when a river catches fire or the cancer rate in a particular neighborhood goes off the charts
or fertile farm land becomes a sandy waste. The average
life span of a Mesopotamian city was about three centuries, because after that, the salinity of surrounding
fields, the result of constant irrigation, rendered them
sterile. Rain water is distilled, but river water carries
with it the minerals that have dissolved in it during its
course from the mountains. Every year of intensive irrigation of the fertile valleys of California shortens their
life expectancy, and the longer the present pattern per-
sists, the harder it will be to ignore its effects.

The main point of this book, however, goes a step
further than that. It can be hard, especially emotionally,
to reconcile the idea of hell with the idea of a loving and
omnipotent God (in theological language, this is referred to as the theodicy problem, which I will deal with
at greater length in the closing chapter). Marilyn Mc-
Cord Adams, among others, argues that it is impossible
to believe that a good and omnipotent God would consign anyone to hell, and I agree.[7] The hell you are going
to be reading about is not a hell inflicted by God on
people who broke the rules. It is not a punishment for

---

7. Marilyn McCord Adams, "The Problem of Hell: A Problem of Evil for
Christians," in *Reasoned Faith*, edited by Eleonora Stump (Ithaca, N.Y.:
Cornell University Press, 1993).

the things they did before they died. It is simply a lot of people living the way they want to live, just as they did before they died. Before they died, their loving Lord was trying to get through to them, making the best of their choices, warding off the worst, and that still holds true after death.

We don't necessarily stop loving children who make a mess of their lives. At our best, we don't give up on them. We may decide that the best thing we can do for them is to get off their backs completely, but our intent in this is not rejection. If our every effort to communicate has only made things worse, then the wisest and most loving thing is to stop trying to communicate for a while. The tough love of AlAnon is truly for the sake of the alcoholic, out of a recognition that all the loving rescue efforts have only reinforced a profoundly destructive pattern.

Granted, the theodicy problem involves not just the notion of a loving God but the notion of an omnipotent God; and as parents or as companions of an alcoholic, we are far from omnipotent. Still, I believe that the problem has been unnecessarily complicated by sentimental notions of the nature of love, assumptions that love would never do anything that causes pain or that love must always give us what we want.

Let me scale the problem down for a moment. I seem to have no trouble reconciling the notion of a loving God with my own failings. Paul cited God's reaching out to us "while we were sinners" as evidence of divine love (Romans 5:8). If this is the case, then the theodicy problem begins to look like one of degree. *How much* evil can be reconciled with belief in a loving God? For some people, the death of a single child is too much—especially if the child is their own. For others, the death of millions in the Holocaust is not too much. Victor Frankl found eloquent faith in the death camp. For many, it must be granted, the idea of an eternal hell is too much, but equally thoughtful people have come to opposite conclusions in this instance as well. To the best of my knowledge, no one has managed to quantify evil; and even if we could, who would decide how much is too much? Who would pick the magic number?

We cannot look at the daily news without at least suspecting that we are capable of choosing evil. When a child is abducted, tortured, and killed; when a man who has lost money day-trading goes on a killing rampage; when one tribe, clan, or ethnic group sets about the systematic elimination of another, it is awfully clear that we are capable of creating hell for each other. What Swedenborg asks you to believe is simply that we are capable of preferring hell to heaven not just from time to time, not just under extraordinary circumstances, but forever—and when you look at how resolute and ingenious we can become in defense of the indefensible, this doesn't seem all that far-fetched.

Can we really hang onto that preference forever? That, for me, is the question. I reject categorically the notion that God would consign anyone to hell for a moment, let along for eternity. That is actually *wanting* someone to be evil and is as demonic as love is divine. But can we ourselves *become* eternally, irredeemably evil? Nobody has been in hell forever yet, but that doesn't mean that nobody will. It's largely a theoretical question until we take it personally. There are several personal ways to ask the question. Can we completely kill our conscience? Can we wound our sanity beyond recovery? Can we so deafen ourselves that even the very voice of God cannot get through to us? Peck suggests that we can. He cites Gerald Vann's statement, "There can be a state of soul against which Love itself is powerless because it has hardened itself against Love."[8] Universalists have always said we cannot—a loving God will make sure that eventually the pain and folly of genuine evil will convert even the hardest heart.

Again, the hell Swedenborg is talking about is simply a place (loosely speaking) where we not only do evil but are in the exclusive company of people like ourselves. It may be a dangerous doctrine, but it is surely a realistic one to recognize that there are times when we *enjoy* evil. That time I lost the ticket to the football game, I was finding quite a bit of pleasure in my self-pity. My late colleague Cal Turley, a pastoral therapist, used to remind us that people behave in neurotic ways because they derive some benefit from it. He insisted that you couldn't deal with their dysfunction until you understood what it was that they were getting out of it.

My father told of trying to help a parishioner who made all sorts of trouble for himself by periodic binge drinking. In his sober times, which I gather were long enough to enable him to function fairly well, he could see what he was doing to himself. Dad talked to him once right after one of his binges and asked him whether he knew why he had gone off the wagon again.

---

8. Gerald Vann, *The Pain of Christ and the Sorrow of God*, cited in M. Scott Peck, op. cit., 73.

His response was, "But I had a hell of a good time." If we cannot admit that there is such a thing as a hell of a good time, we are (a) likely to follow the universalist line of reasoning and (b) be seriously out of touch with reality.

In the framework of Swedenborgian theology, it makes sense that there are "delights of evil." For Swedenborg, evil is essentially a matter of our priorities. In the hierarchy of loves I outlined in the last chapter—love of the Lord, love of the neighbor, love of the world, and love of self—all the loves are good provided they are in that order. Love of self becomes evil, tyrannical, when it is put in first place, when we become so absorbed in it that it drowns out everything else. Love of the Lord does not drown out love of self for the simple reason that the Lord loves us and therefore *wants* us to love ourselves as well as each other: "You shall love your neighbor as yourself" (Leviticus 19:18). For the same reason, love of the neighbor does not drown out love of self. In fact, as we become aware of the reality of other people and of the extent to which we actually internalize them, the whole line between self and other becomes increasingly permeable. We find our boundaries to be movable, not fixed, with some people we let in and others we do not, with times to open the doors and times to close them. We realize more and more the extent to which we are interdependent—in David Bohm's marvelous phrase, "relatively autonomous subtotalities"[9]—and can actually believe that our own happiness is important to others, as theirs is to us.

---

9. David Bohm, *Wholeness and the Implicate Order* (London: Routledge and Kegan Paul, 1980), 179.

Because our own happiness is important, there is pleasure in pleasing ourselves, even when we do so at the expense of others. We would not do these appalling things if they caused us nothing but pain. To imagine Swedenborg's hell, then, is to dismiss all the caricatures, all the images of eternal barbecues, and to look squarely at the nature of the hells we make for ourselves here and now. Their fire is not literal fire, but the fire of anger or hatred. Their torment is not inflicted by God sitting in judgment but by the people who return our hatred with hatred of their own, by the way in which we have set ourselves against reality. It is to imagine communities made up entirely of people wholly wrapped up in themselves, seeing everyone else as enemy. But it is also to admit that sometimes that is just what we are looking for.

I will be looking at this issue more closely in the final chapter, but for now it may suffice to say that the basic Swedenborgian answer to the theodicy problem—the reconciliation between the existence of hell and the goodness and omnipotence of God—is simply that no one is in hell who does not want to be there. I can't simply be "sent" there; I have to buy the ticket and get on the train myself. If at any time I actually wanted to get out, I could. The gates of hell are not to keep people in, but to keep them out. We need to come down from the heights of metaphysical abstraction and take seriously two recurrent features of our own experience—that evil is really bad for us in and of itself, and that we are perfectly capable of enjoying it.

WHO's afraid?

There is more to be said about the nature of evil. Mikhail Kazachkov styled himself as an "evilologist" as a result of his experiences in the Siberian gulag. He criticized Goethe's *Faust* for not recognizing what he insisted were the two salient characteristics of evil, namely, that it is always afraid and that it always lies. I have already paid some attention to evil's inevitable tendency to distort perception, to lie. Kazachkov's basis for insisting on the underlying fear was his understanding of the KGB guards who force-fed him during his hunger strikes and who apparently had the power of life and death over him. They knew, though, that their own survival depended on that kind of complete control. They knew themselves to be hated. They felt themselves surrounded by a will for their destruction. They were governed, controlled, by their fear.[1]

Swedenborg agrees. In *Heaven and Hell* §543, he writes,

> In general, all the people in the hells are controlled by their fears, some by fears they have imposed and eventually internalized in the world; but since these fears are not adequate, and since they gradually lose force, they are controlled by fears of punishments.

To digress for just a moment, let me note again that, in this understanding of hell, the "punishments" are not inflicted by God but by one's compatriots. We are talking about communities made up entirely of individuals who believe that no one else matters except themselves. The constant effort of a loving God is, in fact, to keep the violence within limits, to permit no more than is necessary. Part of the torment of hell is that no one can achieve any lasting dominion. Zero-sum games insist on having losers; and, in the ultimate zero-sum game, every individual is going to lose most of the time.

But let us turn from the hereafter to the here and now. There are two commonly recognized reactions to fear: fight and flight. The equation of flight with fear and fighting with fearlessness is a false ratio. People often fight because they are afraid, because they see something or someone as threatening. Husbands resort

---

1. Mikhail Kazachkov, "What Ever Happened to the Evil Empire?," op. cit., 8–9.

to physical abuse of their wives out of fear—fear of losing control, and especially, one suspects, fear of a desertion that would brand them as worthless in their own eyes, a subject I'll return to later. Parents abuse children out of fear, primarily fear of loss of control in the face of the overwhelming demands that parenting imposes. On the global scale, we have just been through an arms race that neither side could possibly win, that left us with an incredibly lethal heritage of nuclear missiles, out of the belief that the only guarantee of peace (defined at one point as "permanent prehostility") was a balance of terror. With the collapse of the Soviet threat and the consequent downsizing of the fear factor, we find ourselves strangely disoriented. The possibility of peace seems strengthened, but if it is not a balance of terror, what is it?

Physical violence and flight are only the most obvious manifestations of fear. Passive aggression, for example, is a recognized kind of fight. In general, fear gives rise to the perception of the other as the enemy and therefore to malice. Vicious political infighting can take place under the surface of urbanity and courtesy. It happens in academia and in the church as well as in national and local politics. Economic warfare has some strong social sanctions. Manipulative behavior, shifting the blame to others, positioning oneself to get maximum credit, and all sorts of Machiavellian skills can be used as deliberately and heartlessly in family settings as in the world of business. The manifest issue may be status or tenure or power or money. The hidden agenda is the alleviation of fear.

I read some years ago that the long-term successful

con artist will not appeal to his victims' generosity because, when they discover that they have been cheated,
they will have no hesitation in reporting the fact. However, if they have been taken in by the promise of easy
money, they are likely to be so embarrassed by this ex-
hibition of greed and gullibility that they will not want
anyone to know about it. They were trying to outsmart
the system, and they have been revealed as greedy and
stupid. They are afraid of disclosure. In other words,
greed seeks out greed because it knows the workings of
fear.

The Gospel of John puts it bluntly. "And this is the
judgment, that the light has come into the world, and
people loved darkness rather than light because their
deeds were evil. For all who do evil hate the light and do
not come to the light so that their deeds may not be
exposed" (John 3:19–20). The evil are not shut out of
heaven but are invited in. The price of admission is simply honesty to the point of personal transparency. It is
genuinely wanting to be understood. Paul had it exactly
right: "Then I will know fully, even as I have been fully
known" (1 Cor 13:12).

This is a terrifying prospect if we do not want to be
exposed; and this fear like others demands to be denied.
The stronger it is, the more desperately we try to conceal it. We need the illusion of total control, so we
struggle to create a world in which we are the demigod,
authoring a script in which everyone else is given lines
that feed our sense of supreme importance.

Swedenborg talks about a "love of dominion" in
Apocalypse Revealed §802, which can over a lifetime develop into an all-consuming need to be in control. It is

ultimately futile because it is utterly unrealistic. None of us is omnipotent. Hitler built up the most formidable military machine of his time and wound up hiding in a concrete bunker and committing suicide. His "thousand-year-Reich" never came into existence for a single day. Not long ago, the news told of Pol Pot in Cambodia, a man who had tried to make himself safe by slaughtering everyone who opposed him, now terminally ill and hiding in the jungle with his few remaining troops, surrounded by vengeful enemies who were probably eager to have the satisfaction of killing him before he died of natural causes or by his own hand or was brought to justice. In politics, Watergate was the undoing of a president who had just been reelected by a landslide and who, by all usual standards, should have felt perfectly secure. In finance, there was the sorry spectacle of Howard Hughes, clinging to a financial empire that seemed to bring him no peace of mind whatever. The common denominator in these stories is fear, fear of military violence in some instances and of political failure or financial dependence in others.

It is all quite understandable. The one person I know from the inside is myself. Unless I really pay attention to others, I am likely to project my feelings on others. If I want what they have, I will assume that they want what I have. If I feel a need to control them, I will assume that they feel a need to control me. If I am concealing my motives, I will assume that they are concealing theirs, and so on. The more completely I am wrapped up in myself, the less capable I am of really paying attention to them, of trying to gather where they are coming from. They become blank screens on which

I project my fears, and I am trapped in a grim circle. My insecurity colors my perceptions, and my colored perceptions confirm my fears.

The world we live in presents us with rich resources for this kind of self-deception. We look at a surface under which things go on, and it is quite possible to keep them hidden. We can smile outwardly when we are inwardly boiling with resentment. We can be patient and gentle with a spouse or a child when we are tired and at our wits' end.

Further, it is not always easy to figure out what causes what. Things will sometimes go well for us, and sometimes not, despite our best or our worst efforts. This means there is no guarantee that virtue will be rewarded or evil punished in this world of ours. Cancer can strike a devoted mother, while an abusive one stays healthy as a horse. A professional athlete can earn millions of dollars selling ego enhancers to kids who cannot afford them, while a high-school teacher can do wonders for a whole generation of students for as low a salary as the taxpayers can manage. Or cancer can strike the abusive mother, the professional athlete can wind up in disgrace, the devoted mother can find herself blessed by health and friends, and the high school teacher can win the lottery. Virtue is not always unrewarded, nor vice unpunished.

In short, whatever we want to believe about people or about values, we can find evidence to support it. People can and do have radically different convictions about the way the world works, about what matters most, and we seem to have formed the habit of believing that we have been convinced by the evidence. The fact that we have been convinced of some very different conclusions, however, suggests that we are not as passive as we pretend to be. Reality may exert some strong pressures, but nothing actually compels us to look beneath the surface to the realm where there is only one conclusion that can be drawn, where there is no way to beat the system. Pessimism is just as much a leap of faith as optimism, and we guide ourselves through the world as we perceive it; and the world as perceived through the lens of fear is very different from the world as perceived through the lens of love.

There is a vivid image of this in Swedenborg's *Heaven and Hell* §478:9:

> In the spiritual world you can see paths, some leading to heaven and some leading to hell. Good spirits follow only the paths that lead to heaven, . . . and do not even see the paths that lead elsewhere. Evil spirits follow only the paths that lead to hell, . . . and do not see the paths that lead elsewhere— or if they do, they have no desire to follow them.

This description is open to a kind of replication in our own experience. I mentioned in the introduction that, according to Swedenborg, we are residents of the spiritual world right now, a world of our own deeper thoughts and intentions, and that our life after death is this inner world become visible. In given situations, different people here and now do see different "paths" opening up, different ways of responding. One will see a chance to score points, one a chance to shift the blame, one a chance to help out, one a chance to make a sale, one a chance to heal an old hurt—the list could to on and on. Fear will see threats. Nobody sees all the ways there are, but normally we see more than one because our concern for ourselves and our concern for others are both looking for avenues of realization. Professional mediators and facilitators need to be skilled in seeing paths that people cannot see when they are mired in conflict.

For me, one of the most rewarding parts of the 1993 Parliament of the World's Religions was a series of sessions led by the Dialogue Project from MIT. Its goal was not to arbitrate disputes but to enable people on different sides of an issue to express themselves clearly. The project modeled an effort to understand that was contagious, and it was impressive indeed to see a group which had reacted negatively to a particular individual become drawn into the facilitators' effort to understand what he was trying to say and why he was trying to say it. We moved, or were moved, beyond the spontaneous impulse to argue in part because we were convinced that we did not have to abandon our own convictions in order to understand those of others. We moved, or were moved, beyond fear. As a result, we began to glimpse paths of communication that we had been blind to before.

My one contribution to the facilitators came outside of the sessions and consisted of the quotation from Swedenborg's *Arcana Coelestia* (§7298:2), cited in part earlier in a different context:

No one should be instantly persuaded of the truth. That is, no truth should be so confirmed that there is no doubt left. This is because truth impressed in this way is second-hand truth, with no stretch and no give. In the other life, this kind of truth is represented as hard, impervious to the good that would make it applicable. So in the other life, as soon as something true is presented to good spirits by open experience, something opposite is promptly presented, which creates a doubt. This enables them to think about it, to wonder whether it is true, and to gather reasons, bringing the truth into their minds rationally. This gives their sight an outreach in regard to the truth, reaching even to its opposites.

This passage suggests that I should be suspicious of certainty. It runs counter to any theological dogmatism by demanding that we open our minds to views that conflict with our own, that we entertain doubt as to the adequacy of our own comprehension. It suggests that a hallmark of a secure faith is an ability to appreciate other faiths and that the hallmark of an insecure faith is a need to destroy the validity of other views. Swedenborg was not entirely above polemic, but it is worth noting that his severest criticisms were leveled against his own church, against Christianity as it had come to be understood and practiced in his own time.

I hope it is clear by now that I am not opposed to critical thinking, but that my own critiques of materialism and determinism and universalism are compatible with a recognition of their effectiveness within the boundaries of their own domains. I would hope that readers who disagree with the view I am advocating might experience a corresponding appreciation. There is a statement of this principle by William Law that I find particularly compelling:

> Selfishness and partiality are very inhuman and base qualities even in the things of this world; but in the doctrines of religion they are of a baser nature. Now, this is the greatest evil that the division of the church has brought forth; it raises in every communion a selfish, partial orthodoxy, which consists in courageously defending all that it has, and condemning all that it has not. And thus every champion is trained up in defense of their own truth, their own learning and their own church, and he has the most merit, the most honour, who likes everything, defends everything, among themselves, and leaves nothing uncensored in those that are of a different communion. Now, how can truth and goodness and union be more struck at than by such defenders of it? . . .
>
> There is therefore a catholic spirit, a communion of saints in the love of God and all goodness, which no one can learn from that which is called orthodoxy in particular churches, but is only to be had by a total dying to all worldly views, by a pure love of God, and by such an unction from above as delivers the mind from all selfishness and makes it love truth and goodness with an equality of affection in every man, whether he is Christian, Jew or Gentile. . . . He therefore that would like as God likes, and condemn as God condemns, must have neither the eyes of the Papist nor of the Protestant; he must like no truth the less because Ignatius

Loyola or John Bunyan were very zealous for it,
nor have the less aversion to any error, because Dr.
Trapp or George Fox had brought it forth.[2]

That truly "catholic" faith can be so because it is secure.
It has no need to attack other faiths.

In a discussion some years ago, I was asked why,
symbolically, the Holy City had such "great and high
walls" if the gates were wide open night and day. The
answer that leapt to mind was that security and openness
are natural partners. Defensiveness is a sure sign of insecurity. Symbolically, weak walls go with closed gates because they suggest a sense of vulnerability—of fear.

By this criterion, Swedenborg was secure in his
Christian faith, writing in *Divine Providence* §256 that

> [t]he reason Christianity exists only in a minor part
> of the habitable world is that it has not been
> adapted to the intrinsic nature of Orientals the way
> Islam has . . . and a religion that has not been
> adapted is not accepted.

Later in the same book (§326:10), after speaking of the
extraordinary variety of organs in the human body,
which for him was an image of the complexity of heavenly community, he wrote, "Heaven, in order to com-
prise all these elements, cannot be made up of people of
one religion. It needs people of many religions."

Insecurity and fear are so closely allied that I really

---

2. Cited from Aldous Huxley, *The Perennial Philosophy* (New York: Harper
Colophon, 1970), 196–199.

do not know where to draw a line between them. Both compel us to be particularly alert to threats from the outside, and in so doing distort our perceptions. Of course there are threats out there, but they are not the whole story. The insecure husband will see in his wife's behavior, will hear in her words, threats that are not there. Shakespeare's image from *A Midsummer Night's Dream* is apt:

> Or in the night, imagining some fear,
> How easy is a bush supposed a bear.

There is a further complication. Presuming that the people we deal with also have various mixtures of better and worse motives, that they have at least some fears of their own, the risk of self-fulfilling prophecy is very real. Fear-driven behavior tends to arouse fears in others. In contrast, I think of a particularly gentle minister of a generation past. He was totally blind in his later years, much loved and much cared for. Essentially, that is, he lived in a world of loving and caring individuals because his own attitude called forth the most considerate behavior from people around him.

This is a very different world from that of the abusive husband. He is driven by fear. If his wife leaves him, he stands condemned as a sexual failure, psychologically castrated. This fear is fostered by a culture that makes sexual success the prime standard of masculinity, and the seeds are sown in the turmoil of adolescence. To the adolescent heterosexual male, the female is the *mysterium tremendum et fascinans*, the mystery that at once enchants and terrifies—but while it is socially acceptable and even required to acknowledge the attraction, masculinity absolutely forbids acknowledging the terror.

Simply to succeed in getting married provides no solution. In some cases, it seems rather to raise the stakes. Once the honeymoon is over, the couple faces the ongoing task of maintaining a relationship that invariably demands sacrifices. The one thing the husband knows with some confidence is that he is physically stronger than his wife. By using that strength to control her, he accomplishes two things. First, he prevents the desertion that would destroy him, and second, he proves to himself that he is not afraid of her.

Now try to imagine what the wife can do or say to get some message through this wall of denial. Direct confrontation will be interpreted as rebellion, to be met with the only strength he has. Efforts to escape the violence will be interpreted as desertion. Efforts to reassure will be interpreted as subtle efforts to disarm him. Efforts to explain, to communicate, will be interpreted as efforts to control him, to shift the focus from the area of his strength to the area of his weakness. The husband's mind, without conscious intent, will see hidden meanings in everything she does. How hard it is *not* to see the bear!

I would highlight the speed and ingenuity of this process. We probably think of the husband as being a kind of physical animal, not very bright. In fact, highly trained and skilled therapists have very little chance of getting messages through intact unless there is some willingness on the part of the husband. Court-mandated therapy is not promising. The chances of the wife's convincing him of her care for his welfare are almost nil.

The more abusive he becomes, the harder it must be for him to believe in the possibility of a loving and trusting relationship. The more abusive he becomes, the harder it must be to believe that this kind of violence is justified, and the harder he must have to work to maintain his illusion against the mounting pressure of the obvious. I do not know how to address the underlying fear but see little prospect of healing unless it is recognized.

Fear-driven self-aggrandizement breeds self-deception for the simple reason that it has to. In Kazachkov's terms, evil is not only afraid, but it also lies. Each of us cannot be the only person in the universe who matters. If I insist on believing that I am, I have to engage in some major distortion of the facts. Actually, the belief is so absurd that I have to conceal it even from myself.

If I am driven by fear, then, threats are everywhere. The only people who do not threaten me are the ones who rotate around me, so to speak, the ones whom I can experience as extensions of my own ego; and at some level I have to suspect that they cannot be trusted to rotate consistently. I am a little like an astronaut in the shuttle, or better yet, in a space suit. My environment is inherently deadly to my pretensions, so I must at all costs insulate myself from it. Psychologically, I have made the claim that there is nothing out there, and that nothing will annihilate me if I ever let it in.

Granted, I do indeed seem to be the center of my world. I, like you, see the world extending around me. This is not the same as saying that things actually are the way they seem, that I am *the* center of *the* world. That may be the view of infantile omnipotence, of the little friend I played hide-and-seek with, but growing up is supposed to involve gaining some sense of proportion. The evidence mounts that other people are as real as I, perhaps even that they are centers; and if the infantile attitude is to be preserved, it must be deliberately defended.

If I want to impose my view of myself on others, one recognizable strategy is leading a life of exemplary morality. "He was a man who lived for others. You could tell the 'others' by their hunted look." We can use conspicuous virtue as a weapon for the belittlement of others, generosity as weapon for subjugation. Under the guise of offering love and comfort, some clergy have actually been sexual predators. Outward humility can be used in highly manipulative ways. If we want to be self-righteous, it helps to be righteous.

Sometime in the 1960s, a young woman I knew came back from a civil rights rally in tears. She had approached one of the major figures who was there (fortunately, I have forgotten which one, but it was definitely not Martin Luther King) to offer her help and had been brushed off casually, cruelly, as insignificant. If you want to rise to national prominence, you can do worse than choose the noblest cause available and ride it for all it's worth. You may actually do a great deal of good—sort of the inverse of the missionaries who went to Hawaii to do good and wound up doing very well indeed. What happens to the cause if your egotism is unveiled can be sad, and what you do to yourself in the process is equally sad.

In *Divine Providence* §109, a particularly striking passage, Swedenborg paints a picture of this practice:

Sometimes it does seem as though the outward form of our thought were not of the same quality as the inner. This happens, though, because our life's love . . . appoints an agent beneath it, an agent called "the love of means," and charges it to be careful to prevent anything of its own appetites from becoming evident. This agent, then, guided by the ingenuity of its captain [the life's love], talks and acts in accord with civil law, moral reason, and the spiritual principles of the church. It does this so cleverly and ingeniously that no one sees that our actual quality is not the same as that of our words and deeds. Eventually, we veil ourselves so completely that we ourselves can scarcely detect the discrepancy.

In more contemporary terms, we create a persona designed to meet the expectations of whatever world we want to impress, a persona designed to succeed. We can do this so thoroughly and so consistently that, ultimately, we believe we actually are the persona. Again, evil is afraid, and it lies. If it lies often enough, it comes to believe its own illusions.

How do we arrive at some kind of fair assessment of ourselves? Frankly, I doubt that we can in any final sense. We seem to have a remarkable capacity for surprising ourselves, as circumstances bring out strengths and weaknesses that we did not know we had. There are depths of our being, subconscious energies and patterns, that usually show themselves only in dim and ambiguous reflections. For most of us, much of our life is still unlived; and even for the oldest of us, there is an uncertain number of days yet to come, discoveries yet to be made.

Still, the evidence is that, if we actually want to, we can grow in self-awareness, especially if we are not afraid to listen carefully to each other and to ourselves. I need to pay serious attention to the way other people react to me. From the inside, I can see things about myself that they cannot; but from the outside, they can see things about me that I cannot. There is no way that the view from the inside and the view from the outside are going to be identical any more than the views of my two eyes are identical. In both cases, depth of field comes from allowing the differences to interact, from living with the tension. To disregard either my own perceptions or the reactions of those around me can only impoverish my understanding.

In fact, if I am wholly dependent on other's opinions of me or wholly oblivious to them, I am obviously troubled. In the first case, I am constantly looking for approval, pathologically anxious to please. I am blown hither and yon by my desperate efforts to read the minds of people who may actually not be giving me all that much thought. I am so out of touch with others that I cannot really conceive of them as thinking about anyone but me. In the second case, I am just as narcissistic, but my strategy is different. I have nothing to learn from anyone else and will screen out any opinions that differ from my own. In either case, I am functionally incapable of significant relationship, functionally incapable, that is, of living in the world of people around me.

A further thought may be in order. In a criminal trial, the task of the prosecution is to assemble all the evidence that points not only to the defendant's guilt but also to the defendant's destructive intent. The task of the defense is to assemble all the evidence for the defendant's innocence both in fact and in intent. To put it bluntly, the task of each side is to distort as much as possible without actual perjury, on the theory that, out of the clash of these distortions, a true picture will emerge. The ingenuity expended on both sides can be impressive. I'm reminded of the widow listening to the minister's eulogy for her husband. After about five minutes, she leans over to her small daughter and says, "Ellen, slip up front and see who that is in the casket." And in all seriousness, it can happen that a minister works so hard to portray a difficult person in a favorable light that members of the family are left with the feeling that the difficulties they experienced must have been their own fault. Different people do see the same things differently.

In the language of the Gospels, the title of the prosecuting attorney was *satanas*, "satan"; and the title of the attorney for the defense was *parakletos*, the "Paraclete" or in the King James Version, the "Comforter." The evil of fear plays the role of prosecuting attorney to perfection, distorting everything in the direction of condemnation. If "they" disagree with me or stand in my way, if "they" raise awkward questions or give evidence of mistrusting my motives, they are *ipso facto* wrong and must be publicly convicted of that wrong. We are remarkably free to interpret the world as we will.

That is not the whole story. I doubt that this freedom is absolute, believing rather that we are constantly dealing with some interface, some mix, of subjectivity and objectivity. True, no one else sees the world through my eyes, exactly as I do. Conversely, no matter how selective my bias may be, reality offers a limited stock to choose from. Herbert Fingarette has put it very concisely: "The world is multimeaninged. But the world does not have *all* meanings. This would indeed be the end of objectivity. An act may have many meanings, but there are infinitely more meanings which it can be objectively shown not to have."[3] The same person sees different things differently.

Can we keep both of these principles in mind simultaneously—that different people see the same thing differently, and that the same person sees different things differently? Can we live, that is, in a kind of no-man's-land between subjectivity and objectivity? It brings me back once more to my mistrust of certainty. Or to put it differently, if I am in your visual field, you cannot see through me. I impose certain limits on what you can see: in my father's words, I make a better door than I do window. Yet within those limits, you have a very real freedom as to what you will focus on. I can be with people constantly for a full day and retain no memory whatever of what they were wearing. Yet a particular facial expression or gesture can be vividly imprinted, unforgettable. Where does the subjective stop and the objective begin?[4]

---

3. Herbert Fingarette, *The Self in Transformation: Psychoanalysis, Philosophy, and the Life of the Spirit* (New York: Basic Books, 1963), 46.

4. Swedenborg describes this situation quite concisely in *Soul-Body Interaction* §1: "The orderly way is for the thinking mind to flow into the sight, subject to the conditions imposed on the eyes by the objects of vision, which conditions the mind also adjusts to suit itself."

If this is a "multimeaninged" world, then each of us is bound to be selective, as we obviously are. Our selectivity has been shaped by our childhood experiences, by our education, by our peers, by the people we have admired and emulated. It has been shaped by our ambitions, our experiences of marriage and parenting, our social lives. It has been shaped more than we might realize by the ways others perceive us, by the kinds of person whom we tend to attract and the kinds we tend to distance. It is shaped by our loves and by our fears; so it behooves us to recognize the importance of our attitudes.

Underlying this chapter is the premise that through all the ups and downs of everyday living, we develop fundamental, habitual attitudes that have a major and consistent influence on our selectivity. We might compare ourselves to diagnostic instruments, gradually tuned by experience and by repeated choice to pick up particular signals from the cacophony of the world around us. The well-attested effectiveness of the wounded healer testifies to the potential usefulness of our individual sensitivities, and the proliferation of support groups testifies to our recognition that those who have "been there" have a special capacity to understand.

Any and all of these special sensitivities are, in some sense, distortions. They can pick up some very faint signals and amplify them; and this can be immensely useful. The sensitive individual can pick up faint early warning signals that the rest of us would miss completely. Problems arise, though, when we deny that we are amplifying and convince ourselves that the world is exactly as we perceive it. Fear alerts us to threats; chronic fear sees nothing but threats. Unless we recognize what is happening, this cuts us off from others who perceive the world differently, and it cuts us off from much of the world itself. A significant part of becoming truly adult is coming to recognize both the value of our way of perceiving and the limitations of that value. This enables us to become distinctive members of the human community, members with unique gifts to bring and with a recognition of our need of the community to supply what we cannot.

Something we might as well call "reality" tends to keep the pressure on for its recognition. It obviously does not compel perfect acknowledgment, or we would all be in agreement about it; but it does make us work harder and harder to maintain our most disastrous illusions.

We live in a world, then, that leaves us free to call evil good if we so choose, but that exerts a constant pressure toward realism. It is a world that urges goodness but does not compel it. Before we complain too much about its flaws, we might do well to appreciate the love and wisdom implicit in this combination of hope for our wellbeing and respect for our freedom. Perhaps, even though it is so much bigger than we are, we do not need to be afraid of it.

WHat's Next?

Returning to Webster's definition of hell as "the place or state of punishment of the wicked *after death*," we may now focus on the question of individual immortality. As some past Down East philosopher once observed, the death rate hovers at about one hundred percent. Under a materialist construction, that is the end of the story. Countless religious traditions, on the other hand, insist that we survive as individuals after death and that, without this belief, life does not make sense. To the Swedenborgian, spirit is real, spirit is now, and spirit is forever; and these beliefs go together. The materialist hypothesis, effective as it is in its own proper domain, leaves a great deal unexplained, as I hope will become clear as we proceed. It would help, surely, to know whether our lives are a forty-yard dash or a marathon. It might make a difference in how we decide to run the course.

I'm not particularly interested in providing "proof" of our immortality, however, primarily because I think proof is overrated. The essence of proof would seem to be the achievement or the communication of certainty, and certainty has no necessary connection with truth. That is, it is quite possible to be absolutely certain and absolutely wrong. "Certainty" is not what we think about something; it is how we feel about what we think. If certainty and truth have no necessary connection, it follows that a search for truth may lead us away from certainty and that a search for certainty may lead us away from truth. It does seem that the more rigorous philosophy becomes in its quest for certainty, the more arid it becomes. It also seems that the achievement of certainty can blind us to anything that would challenge it.

This takes me back to my college years, to a day when I was home on vacation and went to a service station that had been converted to an auto dealership. The former service bays were now showroom space, with floor-to-ceiling plate glass windows where the big overhead doors had been. Walking face first into a wall of plate glass should be enough to convince anyone that some kind of reality exists whether we perceive it or not, and that you can't always trust certainty.

Perhaps I should pause a moment because, in our everyday lives, we rely on any number of "certainties," and those lives would be unbearably complicated if we did not. If we had to check continually that the law of gravity was still working, that the legs of the chair were still intact, that our hearts were still beating, and so on, we would never have attention left over to give to the maintenance of our own lives, let alone to any of the myriad things we want to do or believe we should do.

Every once in a while, though, one or another of these certainties may be challenged. There is solid glass instead of open air. There is a tremor, and the earth beneath our feet is suddenly not solid. There is a cardiac incident, and the regular, reliable beating of the heart becomes uncertain. The chair collapses underneath us. For all we know about their reasons, solar eclipses can still bring a sense of suspension of reality, a feeling that we cannot really trust the rules. It is a distinct relief when the world brightens again and the birds break their puzzed silence.

This recommends, I believe, a kind of "practical certainty" that stops well short of dogmatism or absolutism. When the evidence points overwhelmingly in one direction, we trust it, but we try to keep our minds open to the counterintuitive hints that can lead to unexpected revelations. When the evidence is ambivalent, we follow what makes the most sense but do not suppress the elements that do not fit. Above all, we try to avoid ego investment in any given explanation. We try to avoid putting ourselves in a position where changing our minds would mean (or feel like) losing face.

At the extreme of academic perfectionism, one does not publish anything that one is not prepared to defend to the death. It is rare indeed to find a scholar flatly retracting something previously published, saying "I was wrong." I recall the sad story of one scholar who, when the Dead Sea Scrolls were first discovered, published the opinion that they should be dated in the Middle Ages. As the evidence mounted against him, he marshalled more and more abstruse arguments in defense of his position, until finally he totally discredited himself.

A similar phenomenon can be found in politics, where there is the matchless opportunity for a president to attribute hard times to the effects of a predecessor's policies and good times to the effects of his own, so that history is revised with each change of administration. It has been amply documented in millennial movements, where time after time predictions of the end of the world have proved wrong, leading usually not to the admission of outright error but to some "slight adjustment" of the theory. In general, the more absolute a church's claims to possession of the full truth, the more ingenuity is needed when one or another of its "truths" proves indefensible.

However strongly we may long for certainty in matters of value—and the growth of fundamentalist churches testifies to the strength of that longing—it is not so easily come by as certainty about gravity and chairs or so widely shared. People can be and are equally certain of quite incompatible theologies. People who have been absolutely certain can change their minds. If certainty closes the mind, if it marks the end of discovery, the end of learning, it should surely be avoided at all costs; and we should seek out instead the blessings of doubt noted earlier.

On theological grounds, then, I do not believe that we can arrive at absolute truth about a matter such as immortality and that, in fact, a measure of uncertainty may be healthy. I do believe we can move *toward* truth, however. It may not be possible to draw an absolutely perfect circle, but we can do a better job with a compass than freehand, and we can tell the difference. There is a sane, solid, and fertile middle ground of rationality that lies between the sterile desert of nihilistic scepticism on the one hand and the morass of naive credulity on the other, and that's where I'm trying to stand.

In a sense, that ground lies outside my personal perspective. The philosopher George Santayana is credited with a saying of which I am particularly fond: "We may never know who discovered water, but we may be sure that it was not the fish." If we are totally immersed in a particular culture, there will be aspects of it we simply cannot see; and these aspects will be the invariant ones, the constants. We are unaware of the pressure of the atmosphere until we change elevation. One of our Swedenborgian clergy spent a year on Mauritius and, when he returned to Ontario, "saw" for the first time things he had never noticed. Seeing planet earth from space has proved to be an experience of revelatory power for any number of astronauts. It is understandable, then, that people who have been immersed in the physical sciences have difficulty seeing those sciences from the outside. Their whole world readily becomes *the* whole world.

The world of physical matter is an incredibly intricate and fascinating one. Our study of it has transformed many aspects of our lives. For millennia, parents could raise their children by passing on the skills they had received from their parents and could do so with perfect confidence that they were preparing their children to meet the challenges of adult life. Now parents turn to their children for help with their computers. It felt strange to me when one of our sons decided to study theology and I realized that I actually had resources that might be of value to him. There might be something I could pass on. It still doesn't feel quite safe. It feels as though his world *ought* to have moved beyond mine.

One side effect of our fascination with science and technology is a subtle devaluing of much of the nonscientific learning of the past. There is talk in academic circles of this being a "postmetaphysical age," an age when one no longer asks the unanswerable questions. There seems to be no limit to discovery in the physical sciences, and, in those fields, achievement is clearly identifiable and often generously rewarded.

What seems to have happened, unfortunately, is that science has tended to believe and to insist that nothing exists outside its boundaries. The materialist hypothesis says, roughly, that if it cannot be weighed and measured or in some manner quantified, it does not exist. This means, of course, that theorems exist only as marks on a page or as sound waves or as patterns of neural activity. It is an assertion that is virtually impossible to apply rigorously to any wide range of human experience, to most of life outside the laboratory. It does not work at all efficiently in describing the phenomena we group under the general heading of "human nature." I find it understandable but very sad that science tends to deny the relevance of questions it has chosen to exclude from its own consideration. This prompts serious questions about the advisability of applying "scientific" methodologies to phenomena that science itself says are unreal.

Having spent most of my life working with human nature, it is very hard for me to take radical materialism seriously. I have only recently come to realize that, if you spend years and years immersed in the study of physical phenomena, it may be genuinely difficult to realize that this is an artificially delimited field. Only recently, in fact, have I found it possible to read the claim that science has made it impossible to believe in the human soul without dismissing the author as mentally deficient.

Scientists themselves are not unanimous on the point. There is a growing sense of convergence of science and mysticism, for example, as science begins to probe realms of uncertainty and paradox. There are the beginnings of an epistemological shift, a shift from viewing the findings of science as conclusions to regarding them as approximations. It begins to appear that the only way to avoid asking the unanswerable questions is to stop asking questions at all, because new answers keep prompting new questions until we reach the ones we cannot handle.

Science and human nature converge with particular intensity in the field of medicine. On the one hand, we have clear demonstrations of the effectiveness of psychotropic drugs. On the other hand, we have the tragedies that occur when people do not take their medications—we have not yet come up with a medication that makes people take medication. We have also the demonstrated effectiveness in many cases of forms of therapy that do not use medications at all, that rely on exchanges of meaning that cannot be weighed or measured. Most pertinently for my present subject, science itself has run into serious problems in the matter of death.

This is a chapter on immortality, and near-death experiences have brought a new element into the discussion. It used to be possible to say with some confidence that no one has ever come back and told us, but now that is open to debate. People who have had NDEs seem to be quite convinced that they have died and come back. They now share a conviction, a kind of unforced confidence, that they are essentially spiritual beings, that they have a personal identity that will continue to function after their bodies finally and irreversibly die. Some people who have not had NDEs argue that if they are now alive, they were never really dead. We have the intriguing phenomenon of redefinition of "death."

Logically, this might be a relatively simple matter. The most obvious solution would be to regard death as a process over a period of time rather than as an instantaneous event and to identify stages in that process. There would be a beginning, when the first vital sign failed, and an end, when the process became irreversible. It might even be possible to identify the space in this process when NDEs can occur and to give it a more precise name than "near-death."

Culturally, things are a little more difficult. The definition of death has been delegated to the medical profession, and the medical profession, in its understandable reliance on the principles of hard science, tends toward materialism. The age-old definition of death as the time when the soul leaves the body will not do. Under materialist assumptions, death is simply the end of the body's ability to function. It is irreversible by definition. This means that anything reversible cannot be death. The actual logic of this is questionable. It is like having "known" that cancer is incurable, discovering a cure, and then deciding that if this can be cured, it cannot be "real" cancer. However, when we deal with death, whether "scientifically" or not, there tends to be an underlying emotional agenda. Especially in our culture, it is not something that people want to talk about.

It is an even more perplexing matter ethically. If hearts are to be salvaged for transplant operations and if it is unethical to take a heart from a living person, then we need a definition of death that will allow removal of the heart before it starts to degrade—a flat EEG, for example. However, it seems that any definition of death that meets this requirement also allows for revival. So we are currently groping around in a territory called "near-death" or "clinical death," which is taken not to be "real death" because it may be reversible, but is dead enough for organ salvage, a rather illogical compromise.

The main value of all this, as far as I am concerned, is not that it provides answers but that it raises questions, that it challenges "certainties." It says that we don't really know what death is. We thought we did, but it turns out that none of our definitions fits all circumstances. Maybe all we can be certain about is taxes.

We may leave this question aside for the moment, though, and look at one part of the NDE experience that says something striking about our nature as human beings, namely, the "autoscopic" experiences that are reported with some frequency. The revived patient tells

of having seen herself lying inert, obviously totally unconscious, with the medical staff working to revive her.
She has seen this from a definite perspective outside her
body, usually up near the ceiling of the hospital room.
She accurately describes people (including such features
as bald spots) and events as seen from that perspective.
Normally, this does not happen until the EKG is flat,
until the heart has stopped, which used to be a sure in-
dication of death. Since NDEs often happen in emergency situations, it is rare that an EEG is involved, but
in a few instances flat EEGs are also documented. It has
long been known that people in comatose states have
heard and retained things said before their return to
consciousness, but this is different. This is visual, and it
is certainly not the physical eyes that are doing the seeing. Further, it seems to occur not in a comatose state
but to be triggered only by what we used to regard as
death.

The particular importance of these accounts is that
their accuracy can be and has been checked. In countless
instances where individuals were unconscious when
brought into the emergency room, they later report who
was tending to them and what was done. The conclusion
seems inescapable that *human consciousness is separable
from the body*, at least briefly. Vision is not absolutely dependent on our eyes, nor thought on our brains. As far
as I am concerned, no account of human nature is now
adequate unless it accounts for these reports. Brief as
they are, they are not easily dismissible. Whether the individuals were "dead" or not, they functioned as individuals in an identifiable locus outside their bodies. They

not only perceived what was happening but retained their sense of identity and their memory.

Once this is granted, the question of immortality needs to be rephrased. One huge obstacle to belief, it turns out, is simply not there. It does seem that I can do without my eyes for seeing and my brain for thinking, at least for a short time. Personality and memory remain intact as well. The question is not "whether," then, but "how long?", and no verifiable way of testing this has emerged. There is no particular scientific reason to believe that this condition does or does not last forever. Immortality may not be proved, but it is much harder than it used to be to claim that it has been disproved.

There are, of course, countless people who have claimed to have experiences of a spiritual world, none, to my knowledge, more remarkable than Swedenborg. In the late 1750s, stories were circulating in Europe about this man in Sweden who apparently had paranormal powers. On one occasion, he had accurately described a fire raging in Stockholm while he himself was at dinner in Gothenburg, on the other side of the country. Some time later, he startled the queen by telling her a secret known only to her and her deceased brother. On still another occasion, he had told a widow where to find a needed receipt by getting the information from her deceased husband.

His claims raised issues that still arise when claims are made for the reality of spirit, and the response to them is worth a brief digression. This man could not be lightly dismissed as a crackpot. He was an active and respected member of the Swedish Parliament. He had until his retirement served with distinction on Sweden's "College of Mines" (the federal bureau that oversaw the mining industry) and had written the definitive work on the processing of iron and copper. He was a nobleman, welcome in the royal court.[1]

It was a time of intellectual ferment, with the conflict between materialism and religious spirituality—the current and the tide—still in the flush of its initial energy. Empirical science was on the rise, and superstitions of all kinds were under attack. Perhaps in reaction to this, there was a lively interest in spiritualism, which could, then as now, take some bizarre forms. Swedenborg, with his credentials in both science and spirituality, was a natural center of attention. Quite understandably, his claims to empirical data on the reality of spirit were controversial, welcomed by some and ridiculed by others.

The philosopher Immanuel Kant provides a case in point. He was asked by an acquaintance to investigate this matter, and he did so. He wrote to this acquaintance, Fraülein von Knobloch, not only that the accounts were attested by highly reliable witnesses, but that a friend's visit to Swedenborg found him to be an open-hearted and rational individual.[2] Four years after this letter, however, Kant wrote and published a little

---

1. Cyriel Odhner Sigstedt, *The Swedenborg Epic: The Life and Works of Emanuel Swedenborg* (New York: Bookman Associates, 1952); and George F. Dole and Robert H. Kirven, *A Scientist Explores Spirit: A Compact Biography of Emanuel Swedenborg with Key Concepts of Swedenborg's Theology*, 2nd edition (West Chester, Pa.: Chrysalis Books, 1997).

2. Rudolph L. Tafel, ed., *Documents Concerning the Life and Character of Emanuel Swedenborg* (London: Swedenborg Society, 1875), vol. 2.1, doc. 272, pp. 625–628.

book that held Swedenborg up to ridicule and virtually destroyed the Swede's credibility in academic circles.[3]

Evidently, what had happened was that his letter to the Fraülein had made him appear to be an advocate of spiritualism and had resulted in "incessant questioning." As a young man trying to establish his credibility for a university post, he could hardly afford to be tarred with this brush. He was well aware that Swedenborg's account of reality was "uncommonly like" his own but felt it necessary to distance himself from it by ridicule rather than to have his own system discredited because of the similarities.[4]

The question is still with us. Swedenborg reports some twenty-seven years of frequent visits to a spiritual world inaccessible to our physical senses. He also offers an truly elegant picture of a physical/spiritual universe, including a penetrating analysis of human nature and growth. Does the essential sanity of his system lend credibility to his extraordinary accounts of spiritual experience, or does the "abnormality" of those accounts undermine the credibility of his system?

Pascal put the question in the form of a wager. If I believe in heaven and hell and am wrong, I have lost little, if anything. If I disbelieve in heaven and hell and am wrong, I risk losing a great deal indeed. Those who have

---

3. Immanuel Kant, *Dreams of a Spirit Seer by Immanuel Kant and Other Related Writings*, trans. John Manolesco (New York: Vantage Press, 1969).

4. Ibid., 81. For a survey of the evidence, cf. George F. Dole, "The Ambivalent Kant," *Studia Swedenborgiana* 10, no. 2 (May 1997): 1–10. For a useful overview of Kant's later views on Swedenborg, see Gregory R. Johnson, "Kant on Swedenborg in the *Lectures on Metaphysics*," Part 1, *Studia Swedenborgiana* 10, no. 1 (October 1996): 1–38; and Part 2, *Studia Swedenborgiana* 10, no. 2 (May 1997): 11–39.

undergone a near-death experience, however, would probably be unimpressed. Time after time, we find that, while they are no longer afraid of death and are conscious of a beauty that awaits them eventually, their focus is on the present. A good life is worth living not for the rewards it will bring after death but for its own sake. An evil life is to be shunned not because of the punishments it will bring after death but for its own sake. Spirit is real to NDErs, and it is *now*.

That, to me, is the place to start. That is the reason for focusing on autoscopic experiences. Whatever terminology one might choose, these experiences assert something immensely important about human nature. In relatively clinical terms, they say that thought is *not* absolutely dependent on the brain. In more colloquial terms, they say that I am, at least to some extent, a spiritual being. In traditional religious terms, they say that I have a personal soul that can exist apart from my body, am a nonmaterial person characterized by sight and hearing and memory and personality. Again, they do not say how long that thought or that being or that soul will endure, but their evidence for the existence of that thought or being or soul is momentous.

The place to start is not necessarily the place to stop. If the soul can outlive the body by even a few minutes, then the balances tip in favor of its immortality. If separation from the body does not destroy it, what does? Swedenborg's accounts cannot be dismissed as unquestionably hallucinatory, as scientifically impossible. They merit a second look from the perspective of that middle ground of rationality that lies between nihilistic scepticism on the one hand and naive credulity on the other.

I would go further. Since the autoscopic experiences indicate that the functioning person, with sensation, feelings, thought, and memory, is separable from the physical body, it is no longer possible to say that personality is simply an epiphenomenon of the activity of brain cells. If indeed matter somehow evolved into a complexity that ultimately produced consciousness, then something has happened that has enabled that consciousness to issue a declaration of independence.

It is not scientific to dismiss this challenge to the materialist hypothesis, even though it is in some respects a prescientific challenge. The only obvious reason for doing so is an investment in that hypothesis that has placed it beyond question. This investment is understandable on the premise of immersion I mentioned earlier, but the history of science indicates that, whenever this happens, the hypothesis is eventually shown to be indefensible. Whether we look at the geocentric universe or the Newtonian atom, we find the same plot, the same story line. This view has worked so well for us that we cannot afford to discard it. I believe it was Max Planck who remarked that sometimes all that is needed for a scientific leap forward is a few funerals—and I gather that the time came when his own funeral was one of the ones needed.

The hypothesis that most readily accounts for autoscopic experiences is that consciousness is the cause rather than the effect of neural activity. I find it intriguing that people who have had NDEs do not seem interested, by and large, in crusading for the cause of immortality. Death has simply ceased to be a big deal for them. They find themselves to be primarily spiritual beings here and now, and that is what matters most. There is no trace of "pie in the sky by and by." There is no escapism, no other-worldliness, for the simple reason that the "other world" is here and now.[5]

My mother was a devoted Swedenborgian; and, when my father died, she felt that her own time had come. After all, she had always been the physically frail one, while he was uncommonly sturdy, a world-class wrestler in his younger days, and still impressively strong in his late seventies. It troubled mother that she kept on living—she really felt that she did not belong here. In her letters (she was living with my older sister in Edmonton, Alberta), there would inevitably be some variation of the theme, "I don't know why I'm still with you."

Then a church convention was scheduled for Edmonton, and I wrote that I would be attending. The tone of the letter that came back was different. She was actually looking forward to something. The next word from Edmonton was from my sister, telling us that mother had died. It was as though mother had been unable to die as long as she felt (contrary to her conscious theological convictions) that the spiritual realm was somewhere else, somewhere in the future. As soon as she felt that it was in her own present, as soon as her "present" came to life, she became able to move there consciously.

The belief I state in my introduction that "we are residents of the spiritual world right now, that it is the

---

5. See Cherie Sutherland, *Reborn in the Light: Life after Near-Death Experiences* (New York: Bantam, 1992), 81–93.

world of our own deeper thoughts and intentions" is central to a Swedenborgian outlook on immortality for a reason. If our own spiritual natures, our own souls, are unreal to us now, we can hardly expect them to come into existence after we die. If, on the other hand, we have begun to experience ourselves as spiritual beings here and now, we have discovered something that is not bound by the laws of physics and does not show on our medical charts. We have discovered that our thoughts and intentions have identity and personality, that they involve perception and response, that they have a kind of mobility in a kind of environment. We discover that they are substantial in the sense of being resistant to change and in the sense of being able to effect results.

If the stringent rules of physical biology do not apply to those thoughts and intentions, what rules do apply? Experientially, it is clear that our bodies follow a more or less predictable curve. There is the explosive growth of infancy and youth. There is the transition of adolescence, and there are the years of young adulthood, a kind of leveling off of the curve. There is the downslope of middle age, followed by the accelerating decline of the senior years, and there is eventual death.

Experientially, it is equally clear that the "curve" of our intentions is not so predictable. A particular individual comes to mind, a tiny woman who was in her eighties when I knew her. Elsie McLaughlin had, I believe, been one of the first women in this country to become an M.D., so one could presume a history of intense determination and energy. In her eighties, she looked as though it was not safe to let her out in a light breeze but, to borrow from some anonymous source, "she had a whim of iron." This was a *strong* woman. There was nothing whatever frail about her mind or her resolution. There was no sign of a spiritual down-slope. If one were to project *that* curve, it would head off the chart and into eternity.

If, on the other hand, her personality had been an epiphenomenon of her body, one would expect the opposite, a weakening of personality, a dulling of consciousness. After all, the decline had been going on for more than forty years. This weakening, this dulling does seem to happen in some cases, which raises two questions. Why does it seem to happen in some cases, and why does it not seem to happen in all cases?

Under a materialist hypothesis, the answer to the first question is simple. It does not simply *seem* to happen, but really does. The brain deteriorates, so the personality does. The second question, as indicated already, is the one that poses problems. Even when there is no marked deterioration of the brain, there is a dulling of the senses. Sight, hearing, taste, smell, and touch all lose vividness. Muscles lose strength. "I can run as fast as ever, but it takes me a lot longer to get there." There should be an irresistible cumulative effect, and there simply is not. There are too many people who blossom intellectually, emotionally, and spiritually in their "declining" years.

Under the hypothesis that spirit is primary and body secondary, the second question presents no problem. We are engaged in a process of "soul-making." Our decisions make a difference. Essentially we tend toward one form or another of self-definition, and that definition tends to become clearer and clearer, more and more decisive, as the years go by. As muscles that are exercised grow stronger, so mental and emotional abilities are strengthened by their consistent use.

The answer to the first question is not far to seek, either. If the spirit does act through the body, and the body fails in essential ways, then the *activity*, the *self-expression*, of the spirit will be impaired. There are thousands of analogous situations. Just because a transistor fails in my television set does not mean that it is not receiving programs. It simply cannot display them on the screen. Just because the fuel pump fails on my tractor does not mean that my interest in mowing the lawn is dead. I simply cannot execute it as effectively. If Alzheimer's disease fouls up the circuitry of my brain, I may still be trying to send coherent signals—there is little way for the outside observer to know. If you took the best driver in the world, gave her an urgent errand to do, and put her in a car with a fun-house windshield and controls that scrambled themselves at random, she would drive like a maniac. She would be in there trying brilliantly to cope, but the results would be incoherent.

The closest friend of my teen-age years contracted early Alzheimer's and, with a vigorous heart and lungs and the skilled and faithful care of the Veterans' Administration, lived totally incommunicado, under heavy sedation, for years. As long as he was capable of any kind of communication at all, though, the will to communicate was clear, as was the intensity of his frustration. You could not be with him without feeling the strength of his effort to fight through the obstacles, without marveling at his ingenuity in coping with them. Above all, his style remained intact as long as there was any way at all of expressing it. When he could no longer frame intelligible words, he could still quack at a passing duck, and he did. His personality was not dying, not at all.

In short, I would argue that the hypothesis of the reality of spirit offers consistent answers to both questions, while the hypothesis of the sole reality of matter does not. The scientist is supposed to go with the hypothesis that works best in the most cases. In fact, the scientist is supposed to welcome the case that defies the current hypothesis, since this is exactly what opens the door to discovery. The fact that light acts like waves and like particles at the same time should be more exciting than distressing. So too should be the fact that consciousness is separable from the body and the brain. So too should the blossoming of personality during years of physical decline.

The hypothesis of the reality of spirit does challenge the determinism that is often allied to materialism and that has demonstrated such impressive explanatory power. Science has accomplished wonders by tracing back causal chains, by learning how things happen. Determinism as a philosophical stance simply maintains that this kind of causality is the only kind that exists. There is, in a sense, no way to change the course of events because everything that happens has definite causes in the past. It is a severly rational position and a severely limiting one.

It does not take much reflection to realize two things. First, strict determinism reduces our lives to meaninglessness. I can do only what I am predetermined to do, believe only what I am conditioned to believe. It is absurd to talk about the truth of determinism because it cannot be more than what I am obliged to believe. Others may be equally obliged to disbelieve it, and there are no grounds for negotiation between us. Second, it soon becomes clear how much that is vital to us is not explained by determinism. When a friend of mine was killed by a hit-and-run driver some ten years ago, I found myself asking why. He was a particularly gentle and thoughtful person, a significant asset to his community.

The deterministic answer was very simple and totally unsatisfactory. If a car hits a person hard enough, it causes irreparable damage. My "why," though, looked toward the future rather than at the past. What was the point of this death? Could any good come of it? Gradually, it dawned on me that, in one sense, there was no answer to this question because it depended on how people responded to the event. They might learn not to take life for granted so casually, to treasure themselves and each other more. They might become cynical or embittered or depressed. The future-oriented "why" was an unanswerable question that ought not to be avoided.

We should not avoid the past-oriented questions either. If we do not ask the materialistic questions, the questions of past causes, we fail to learn what might help us prevent future deaths. If we do not ask the questions of purpose, we lose an opportunity to find the kind of meaning that makes our lives worth living.

I must confess to finding the scientific resistance to the concept of purpose puzzling. I have already suggested that the rigorous enforcement of this resistance would lead to some extraordinary verbiage. It would no longer be possible to say that scabs form in order to protect wounds while new skin develops, that insects emit pheromones in order to attract mates, or that animals hunt in order to find food. Dogs do not want to get outside to relieve themselves, nor do cats want to find shelter from a downpour. The language of purpose is both simple and efficient in any number of instances; and if we regard the function of science as descriptive rather than prescriptive, that simplicity and efficiency recommend themselves highly.

Then too, the materialist hypothesis demands at least one major leap of faith. The notion that human beings are the result of totally random physical events boils down to the claim that, if you have enough little instances of utter senselessness, utter stupidity, they add up to an Einstein. No one, I am quite sure, has succeeded in assembling subatomic particles into a conscious entity, let alone replicating this in accord with standard scientific practice. Even if it were achieved, it would obviously not be the result of random events. A massive amount of purpose and intelligence would have been necessary. No, the hypothesis remains hypothetical, and a rigidly held hypothesis is nothing more nor less than a dogma. It is all very well to say that, if you gave enough monkeys enough typewriters and enough time, one of them would come out with intelligible prose. I'm still waiting for this to happen by accident.

In summary, I find persuasive indications that we are spiritual beings here and now and that we can function as coherent individuals separately from our bodies. This shifts the burden of proof for anyone who would categorically deny the possibility of immortality, and I simply cannot imagine where the evidence against that possibility is going to come from. I hope the thoughts to be be presented in subsequent chapters will strengthen a sense that the notion of immortality, including a heaven and a hell, not only makes sense, but makes constructive sense.

One last point needs to be made before we press on toward hell. There is no question in my mind that the idea of immortality has been disastrously misused. It has been used, that is, to induce people to accept injustice here and now because there will be justice in the hereafter. It has been used to manipulate people into loyalty to the church, often at a ruinous financial cost. It has been used as a foundation for fanatical self-sacrifice, for martyrdom, and for callousness in the face of tragedy.

In the mystery novel *Tuesday the Rabbi Saw Red*, Harry Kemelman's Rabbi David Small draws the following contrast:

> Basically, Christianity is a mystical religion and offers the psychological satisfactions mysticism affords. It is other-worldly, heaven-oriented, while our religion is this-world oriented. We oppose what is evil in the world and enjoy the good things, spiritual and material, it has to offer. We do not shun the world by asceticism or try to rise above it by mysticism, which has no following among the main body of Jews.[6]

6. Harry Kemelman, *Tuesday the Rabbi Saw Red* (Greenwich, CT: Fawcett Publications, 1973), 200.

The Swedenborgian heaven and hell, however, do not lend themselves to this kind of contrast, the reason being that, as already noted, they represent simply the unveiling of the inside of the present. Far from comforting me with the thought that I will be rewarded after death for my faithfulness and that the people I now envy will then be envying me, the basic Swedenborgian view presses me to a deeper and more honest examination of my own deepest values and commitments. It undercuts my tendencies to shape the world to my own convenience, to use my selectivity to gratify myself, and impels me to face what I am doing to myself and to others.

The rest of this book will assume that we do go on living as distinctive individuals after physical death. This assumption, I firmly believe, is more defensible than the assumption that we do not. Such evidence as we do have points toward it rather than away from it. If indeed it makes constructive sense out of our present circumstances, if it offers a coherent understanding of what gives our lives present meaning, that may be reason enough for refusing to dismiss it out of hand.

aRe tHese my kiNô of foLks?

If God does not consign us to hell, then how do we get there? It is all very well to say that we choose to go there, but that broad statement begs to be filled in with some substantive detail. In keeping with the theme introduced in the introduction, the picture Swedenborg offers can, I believe, be tested against our own experience.

We naturally gravitate toward people who share our values and who want to play by our rules. It is no fun to play Monopoly with someone who wants to help you win. We gather voluntarily into communities of interest—business, academic, athletic, or ideological communities, communities concerned with alcoholism, weight loss, bereavement, or parenting teens—where we share common goals and speak a common language. To "share common goals" is to have similar values, to regard the same things as beautiful. I recall thumbing through a book on Las Vegas by someone who referred to it as heaven on earth, and certainly thousands of people gravitate there. The only time I have been there, incidentally, was to attend a conference on metaphysical religions, and my overpowering impression was that there was no place I had ever been where the question of reality versus illusion was more persistently posed.

Hell, for Swedenborg, is wherever people gather who regard themselves as being of supreme importance, of exclusive value. It would be too much to say that they understand each other, but they do at least talk the same language. They strive for "the same" goal in the sense that each strives for supremacy. It is hell rather than heaven simply because, as already emphasized, the success of any one is the failure of all others; but that is the rule that they have accepted. Its residents might very well call it "heaven," because it is what they have decided is good. They "eviled" before death by consistently denying the validity of any desires but their own, and they continue to make this kind of choice in the spiritual world, with some subtle differences that I'll get to later.

There is more to it than that. In chapter 2, I referred to Swedenborg's observation that our fears of social consequences tend to restrain us from acting out some of our more destructive impulses. Immediately after death, he says, we enter a realm ("the world of spirits") where those restraints are successively relaxed. The basic effect of this is that we lose the ability to pretend, that the "agent" of *Divine Providence* §109 ceases to control our behavior. Here in this life, we can gratify our egos by espousing quite noble causes, concealing our egotism even from ourselves. There, our actual motives are obvious, because "there" is our present inner world. If I am egotistical, it is the world of my egotism.

This is the main theme of a full chapter in Swedenborg's *Heaven and Hell* (chapter 52, "Our Second State after Death"). It is, for him, the essential mechanism of judgment. When we become insensitive to the physical world, where "things are seldom what they seem," we become sensitive to a world where we can see what spirit looks like. If there is rage within us, then we have no physical body we can compel to smile, no physical vocal cords which we can force to make placid tones. In some respects, this is like the world of our imagination, where there seem to be no reasons to pretend. In other respects, it is like having the world of our imagination brought out into the daylight.

This means that there is no longer anything superficial about the associations we form. The maxim that "politics makes strange bedfellows" is no longer apposite. In our physical world, in order to do something as simply as buying groceries or getting to work, we may regularly be close to people whose values are radically different from our own. People who live in big apartment buildings know that they have to be careful about granting access to their neighbors because once the barriers are down, the physical proximity of an unwelcome individual can be oppressive.

Where there is no physical world, only a spiritual

one, there simply cannot be this kind of discrepancy between physical nearness and spiritual remoteness. Essential affinity is presence, and essential incompatibility is distance. There is nothing arbitrary about the imagery we use when we talk about "close relationships." Family counselors know the value of social diagrams that have little to do with physical geography. In fact, sometimes the controlling will in a family situation is the will of someone who is not physically present, who may even be dead.

Almost by definition, the superficial is transient, and the essential is constant. This means that the associations we form in the essential world, the world of spirit, will be durable ones. Just how durable is, of course, open to debate; and, as noted in the second chapter, no one has been in hell forever yet. However, it is observable here and now that it is far easier to change strategies than it is to change basic goals, far easier to change recipes than to change tastes. What would be involved in changing the very central purpose of one's life, a purpose rooted and nourished by a lifetime of decisions? What is involved in learning to like someone who really seems unlikable?

The vanishing of the physical world has another effect, as Swedenborg experienced it. What he describes is a kind of shift in the relationship between subjectivity and objectivity. On the one hand, when "There is nothing covered up that will not be uncovered, and nothing secret that will not become known" (Matthew 10:26), major obstacles to accurate, objective perception would seem to have been removed. On the other hand, the inner world that comes to light is our subjective one. If we have inwardly found evil attractive, it will *look* attractive to us. This, in turn, means that people who look evil, people who look "bad," will look attractive to us.

This leads to what may be one of Swedenborg's most dangerous doctrines, namely, that "in its own light," hell can be immensely attractive.[1] Generations of Christians have been urged to stay on the straight and narrow path by the fear of hell. Generations of Christian preachers have worked the theme in spectacular fashion. If there is any single image of hell that pervades religious consciousness, it is the image of torment by fire. Just as horns and a tail mark the cartoon Satan, flames identify the locale. I am inordinately fond of Amos Starkadder's image in *Cold Comfort Farm*:

> "Ye know, doan't ye, what it feels like when ye burn yer hand in takin' a cake out of the oven or wi' a match when ye're lightin' one of they godless cigarettes? Aye. It stings wi' a fearful pain, doan't it? And ye run away to clap a bit o' butter on it to take the pain away. Ah, but" (an impressive pause) *"there'll be no butter in hell!"*[2]

If, though, the spiritual world is the uncovering of our present inner world, we need to allow for the fact that resentment and malice can be attractive to us. We can bask in the flame of rage. I am sometimes inclined to fault Swedenborg for so often describing hell not as it looks to its inhabitants but as it looks "in the light of

---

1. See, for example, *Heaven and Hell* §§131 and 585, *Arcana Coelestia* §4798, *Marriage Love* §§264 and 505, and *True Christian Religion* §80.

2. Stella Gibbons, *Cold Comfort Farm* (New York: Penguin Books, 1983), 98.

heaven." It is all too easy to forget his reminders that it may be quite glamorous in its own light and to rest easy in the confidence that we would never choose anything so ugly and painful.

Actually, if evil is its own punishment, then there is really no more reason to fear hell than there is to fear our own malice. Judging by the range of our own tastes, hell is not all ugliness, not constant fire and brimstone, to anyone who has chosen to live there. Here and now, people flock to horror films. Dracula is usually a handsome devil. If resentment is inherently ugly, if brutality is inherently bestial, then to the mind that enjoys resentment or brutality grotesque creatures look handsome. If home is where the heart is, if money can't buy happiness, then to the mind that treasures opulence, *its* spiritual hovels will look like palaces and *its* spiritual poverty like treasuries of gold or jewels. As mentioned earlier, the values that appeal to us when we are at our best seem foolish when we are at our worst. The values that look ugly to us when we are at our best are immensely attractive to us when we are not.

"In heaven's light," things appear as they are, but what happens if we turn away from it? Even in this re-calcitrant world, clever lighting can lend enchantment to settings that in daylight are simply tawdry. The trouble is, of course, that you have to shut out the daylight. It takes a constant effort to maintain the illusion against the force of reality. This is a significant factor in our choice of company. We seek out people who tell us that we are right and shut out people who tell us that we are wrong. I suspect that nothing is more comforting to the neo-Nazi than to be in the secret room, curtains drawn and blinds closed, surrounded by symbols of the faith, with anyone who would challenge that faith excluded.

In a less dramatic vein, I recall an evening in my college days when I happened to notice the color contrasts of the windows of the quadrangle. The ones lit by incandescent fixtures were obviously yellowish, the ones with flourescent lighting were just as obviously bluish. Yet an observer in any single room would unconsciously adjust to the distortion and would "see" normal hues.

In more fundamental respects, we are likely to be oblivious to things that are constant because our attention is drawn to change. In a seminary course on homiletics, I was advised that the eye and the mind are both attracted to motion so that, if in the same church there is a fly that is moving and a sermon that is not, there is little doubt where the attention of the congregation will be. The corollary of this is that the more constant any factor is in our lives, the more difficult it is for us to recognize it, as evidenced by George Santayana's fish. To quote a college classmate of mine who came back East after years of living in Tucson, "I'd forgotten how water just runs along the ground."

One of my own most vivid experiences along these lines was when as a seminarian I made my first visit to a mental hospital, beginning a Clinical Pastoral Education course. As I walked through the grounds looking for the building where the class was to meet, I realized that I did not know how to read the behavior of the few individuals I could see, and I did not know how they might be reading mine. Were they patients or staff? Where was this particular person in his or her day? Was I seen as an outsider or an insider, envied or resented? Was my anxiety obvious, or did I look arrogant? After all, I *was* anxious, and I did know that I would be free to leave when the session was over. It felt as though I could take nothing for granted.

This remains in my mind as an example of the power of the familiar. There is a sense of freedom in being "at home," in knowing effortlessly where things are and what they mean, what signals are appropriate and how to send them. Hamlet, even under oppressive pressure, joined those of us who "rather bear the ills we know than fly to others that we know not of," deciding not to risk the dreams that might come in the sleep of death.

The judgment Swedenborg describes, then, has these two components. First, there is the discarding of masks, the disclosure of hidden agendas. the emergence of the essential person. Second, there is the natural gravitation of like to like in a world where the only kind of closeness is affinity of character. There is the spiritual homecoming, the discovery of a community of shared values.

The whole notion of judgment as a kind of courtroom procedure, followed by sentencing and punishment for evils, harkens back to the way we used to be, before death, when we were restrained from violating social codes by our fear of the consequences. It betrays what I would call a lack of belief that evil is really bad. Under the plausible surface of the courtroom image lies our own dangerous feeling that evil would really be pretty *good* if we could only get away with it, that the real problem is simply that we are eventually going to get caught and clobbered. From a Swedenborgian perspective, hell is no more a punishment for evil than death is a punishment for cancer. Evil is bad for us. That is why a loving creator tells us to stay away from it.

Swedenborg's way of expressing this general principle is characteristically direct. "The Lord does not punish anyone: demonic society itself does" (*Arcana Coelestia* §245). Or again, "The Lord does not throw anyone into hell. Spirits [that is, we ourselves after death] throw themselves in" (*Heaven and Hell* §545). Scott Peck says almost exactly the same thing, with apparently equal confidence: "God does not punish us; we punish ourselves. Those who are in hell are there by their own choice."[3]

We are not talking about some kind of Faustian bargain with the devil, some single choice of eternal hell. We are not talking about the opposite notion either, some instantaneous rebirth that secures a place for us in heaven forever. We are talking about the effects of a lifelong process of deep-level character formation, about the cumulative effects of daily choices, about "soul-making."

Surely no one could deny the attraction of heavenly community, could resist its beauty. So it might seem, but that is not the way it works, as Swedenborg understands Scripture. As we saw, according to John 3:19–20, light came into the world, but the evil preferred the darkness to cover their wicked deeds. The evil are not shut out of heaven; rather, they are invited in—but at a price. Again, the price of admission is simply honesty to the point of personal transparency. It is genuinely wanting to be understood. Paul had it exactly right: "Then I

---

3. *People of the Lie*, op. cit., 67, n. *.

will know fully, even as I have been fully known" (1 Cor. 13:12).

This means that, to the extent that we are attracted by hell, we feel repelled by heaven. The perceptiveness of genuine love is experienced as threatening. In his *Pilgrim's Regress*, C. S. Lewis offers the allegory of being imprisoned in a cave in the presence of a giant (by the name of Freudian psychology) whose gaze rendered him transparent.[4] He could see the workings of all his inner organs and was appalled. The transparency was experienced as deliberately degrading, but it is clear that the giant's intent is to degrade. By contrast, there is no sense of condemnation emanating from the "being of light" in an NDE. Still, there is the experience of utter transparency, and, whatever the intent of the "light," fear demands to be denied.

Fear demands to be denied, and the stronger it is, the more desperately we try to conceal it. We do not wait until after death to start. Here and now, we may feel the need of a sense of total control over everything that might oppose us and, out of the ambiguities of our circumstances, create that world in which we are demigods. When we do author a script in which everyone else is given lines that feed our sense of supreme importance, there is no way we can be ourselves in a world where there is consciousness of an actual deity, no matter how benign, how lovely, how tolerant, that deity may be. There is no way we can be ourselves in a world where

---

4. C. S. Lewis, *The Pilgrim's Regress: An Allegorical Apology for Christianity Reason and Romanticism* (London: Geoffrey Bles, 1950), 60f.

there are real people with real thoughts and opinions that might not agree with our own.

In a talk given at Harvard some years ago, Huston Smith made a remark that has stayed with me ever since. Its general import was that, by relying on the methodology of the "controlled experiment," hard science has effectively confined itself to the study of what it can control. There is no rational way to extend this to the assumption that, what science cannot control therefore does not exist, although this is the basic assumption of strict materialism.

To extend this image only slightly, if I am governed by fear and by the need to be in control, I need to find an environment in which everything is less powerful than I. If, in fact, I am only a minute speck in a vast universe, "reality" does not offer any such environment. I have to retreat to a world of illusion. I have no real choice. On the other hand, the truth makes us free (John 8:32) because it orients us to the way things actually work. It opens us to the world around and opens the world around to us. Evil (or "sin" in John 8:34) enslaves because it confines me to a world of my own construction, and that world is necessarily minute— necessarily, again, because it has to be smaller, less powerful than I am.

If I am to function in this world of ours, the world I construct must bear some resemblance to the worlds the people around me experience. It is immensely difficult to maintain a view that no one else shares. People who do this tend to wind up in mental hospitals. Of course, if I am "in the cultural mainstream," I will not have to look far for support. The more my world differs from that mainstream, however, the stronger will be the pressures to find kindred souls (a process which is becoming more efficient through the internet) and to confine myself to their company.

The need for support is quite legitimate, and it can lead to the gathering of kindred souls for very worthwhile purposes. I happen to be on the fringes of the formation, greatly aided by computer links, of a support group for adults with congenital heart disease. This responds to a need that did not exist until medical technology enabled infants with serious heart defects to survive at least into early adulthood. Those who do survive experience the world differently from people with healthy hearts, and it is lonely to live in a world where no one shares your view, no one understands what difficulties you live with hourly, no one knows how this interface between the fact of youth and the fragility of life feels. There is no need to invent a world of shared values, no need to go looking for facts that support their shared view. It seems as though they have little choice but to be realists in respect to their physical situations.

It would be irresponsible to leave the topic of finding our cultural home without at least touching on one further question: how "realistic" is our mainstream culture? I have already hinted that the right wing tends to see our country as having a perfect system being abused by immoral people, while the left wing tends to see essentially beautiful people being distorted or even destroyed by a deeply flawed system. I trust it is clear that I would see both the individuals and the system as mixtures of good and bad. It strikes me as ironic, for example, that 1929 did not teach us that an immaterial faith in the power of money is, in fact, more powerful than "material" money itself, that in the 1980s we could bask in the belief that a just society could be founded on greed.

I suspect that the system tends to reflect the values of the individuals who participate in it and that a government or a policy that varies too much from a kind of national average morality either upward or downward has little chance of survival. Prohibition had no chance of success, and contemporary efforts to curb collegiate drinking face an uphill struggle. Ronald Reagan rode rather than created a wave of change. Jimmie Carter lost, I believe, because he was a distinct cut above the prevailing moral norm, and Richard Nixon resigned because, in his handling of the Watergate affair, he revealed himself as distinctly below it. Much of the country treated Bill Clinton's escapades as juvenile rather than as destructive and was clearly out of sympathy with the moral foundations of the prosecutor's zeal.

In the other direction, the mixed nature of our culture (and obviously of the other cultures we can observe) offers differing individuals all different kinds of material out of which to construct smaller worlds to their own liking. The judgment process that Swedenborg describes as taking place after death is best seen as a making manifest of a process that is happening under the surface now—the gravitation of like to like.

One final observation. Swedenborg made the radical claim that he witnessed a "last judgment" in the year 1757 and added to this claim the surprising footnote that it would not make any great difference on the surface. The main change, he said in *The Last Judgment*

§73, was that there would be a new freedom of thought in regard to spiritual matters. If I put this together with his view of the judgment process itself, then what is often portrayed as the decline of moral values in our own times takes on a very different cast. It becomes an earthly version of the same relaxation of external restraints that enables hidden motivations to surface and be dealt with. We are seeing how our ancestors would have behaved if they could have gotten away with it. This includes the "family-oriented" Victorians whose prosperity was built on the silent exploitation of child and immigrant labor; the centuries in which women were regarded as the property of their husbands; and, of course, the millennia in which war was glorified as noble and slavery was taken wholly for granted.

At the close of the 1993 Parliament of the World's Religions, the Dalai Lama made the startling statement that he expected the next century to be notably better than the past one. At the time, I was full of research into the 1893 Parliament and acutely aware of the optimism of that era, an optimism that a century's hindsight reveals to have been naive. The Dalai Lama's statement leaves me wondering whether we, in our fears for the future, are not equally short-sighted, victims of naive pessimism.

What do we have to go on? It has become fashionable, at least in academic circles, to disallow any theory of inevitable progress, but how on earth can we be sure? I would not only grant but insist that technological progress can be a blessing or a curse, but more has changed in recent centuries than our technology. I suspect in fact that most of us would find it far easier to adjust to the technology of the nineteenth century than to adjust to the attitudes—especially if we had the misfortune to be second- or third-class citizens. I suspect that we would be as appalled as was Charles Dickens at the social ills, at the chasm between what was preached in overflowing churches and what was practiced in the streets. I still wonder that the winsome Swedenborgian who fathered that 1893 Parliament of Religions, Charles Bonney, could believe that the twentieth century would see the coming of the kingdom of heaven on earth when he had spent his life fighting against blatant political corruption and corporate greed. Perhaps it was simply because his vision of ideal human society made so much sense that he could not believe that it would not spread.

wHat's HeLL
ReaLLy Like?

When it comes to describing the hells as Swedenborg observed them, we face the problem already mentioned, the problem of a kind of radical subjectivity. We are asked to believe that the various levels and regions of hell are appallingly squalid "in heaven's light," but quite glamorous in their own light. This does not strike me as at all preposterous in view of our human capacity for seeing things the way we want to see them, but that too has been discussed already. The descriptions that follow can perhaps best be read as descriptions of our own inner landscapes, of the mental/spiritual environments we select for ourselves. We do see these inner landscapes differently depending on our moods. What has a glamorous appeal to us on Monday may look quite cheap on Tuesday.

It is wholly characteristic of Swedenborg that he distinguishes three basic levels of hell. This rests in the fact that he sees our human process as consisting of an ongoing interaction among intention, thought, and act (which are, again characteristically, "distinguishably one"). He sees this "trinity" as structuring the spiritual world as well. So the first—and mildest—hell comprises people who are focused on behavior, the second comprises people who are focused on the workings of the human mind, and the third and most vicious comprises people who are focused on the workings of the human heart. The first are the people who will break your kneecaps if you don't pay up, the second are the people who will con you out of everything you own, and the third are the people who will work on your feelings until you have no will of your own. Read M. Scott Peck's description of Hartley and Sarah.[1]

Let us tour these environments in that order, and let me set the description in the first person plural both to keep the language unselfconsciously inclusive and to resist any tendency to put hell "out there," in some remote future. I hope it also conveys the message that there is no assumption of distance between author and reader.

When we are in the FIRST HELL, the rules are very simple. Everyone else is supposed to do what we want them to. We are totally insensitive to their motivations

---

1. *People of the Lie*, 108–120.

because we are totally insensitive to our own. We are the quintessential behaviorists, with the significant limitation that we have no sense whatever of anything like "the common good" or "human rights" or "equal justice." All we know about other people is that they are trying to control us, and the only way to prevent this is to be stronger than they are.

This forces us, reluctantly, into alliances. If things get bad enough for us, if we are sufficiently oppressed, we find ourselves joining with others who suffer in the same way. It is not sympathy that brings us together, but a common resentment or hatred of a common enemy. I would call attention parenthetically to the disorientation in our own country that has followed the collapse of the Soviet Union. With no common enemy of sufficient stature to compel attention, we must either fall apart, invent a new enemy, or find something affirmative that we hold in common. Check out George Orwell's *Animal Farm*.

The third option, finding something *affirmative* that we hold in common, is not really available in hell. The only thing that we all have in common there is our sense of supreme self-importance. There are no diplomats among us, no counselors trained in conflict resolution. There are no honest workers, no devoted parents or teachers or friends. There is absolutely no one we can trust, not for a moment, not even a philosophical bartender. We are sustained in our determination by those times when we are part of an alliance that is in control; but any such alliance is both internally unstable and externally the focus of growing resentment and hatred. We are far too insensitive to moderate the brutality of our oppression, so we simply meet resistance with all the force we dare to exert. Conflicts inevitably escalate until we are overwhelmed, a new alliance takes shape in the ensuing chaos, and we find ourselves among the oppressed. We remember, though, the time when things were as they should be, when we were in control, and we nourish ourselves with the determination to set things right again. We have, above all, an invincible conviction that we are right. What we want is good, and what we think is true.

I'm afraid the illustration that comes immediately to mind is the Balkans, at least as portrayed in the media. We seem to have a situation there in which each party can look back to a time when it was at its zenith and evidently regards that as the norm, the way things are meant to be. Every decline from that zenith is therefore an injustice that must be avenged, a score that must be settled. The futility, the absolute folly of all this is buried under the weight of conviction that "we" are right and that right must triumph, strengthened by romanticized memories of how wonderful it was before things went wrong, memories that translate effortlessly into dreams of future glory. True heroism is sacrificing oneself to the cause, identifying with the collective so completely that one's individual identity disappears—or more accurately, so that the collective is nothing more than the extension of one's own ego.

But back to the behavioral hell. As its residents, we are really not very bright, not at all. Because we are totally insensitive, we are actually incapable of subtlety. We have a vastly exaggerated estimation of our own strength in addition to that blind assumption of our own rightness. We are deafened to each other by our unquestioned assumption that we have nothing to learn. Not only do we know the score, we are the only ones who do. Other people are nothing more than cardboard figures to us, and we are totally incapable of believing that we are the same to them. I'm reminded of a story a student once told me. Her car heater wasn't working, and when she arrived home one particularly cold day, her first words to her elderly mother were, "My feet are frozen." Her mother's response was, "No, they're not. I was just outside, and it's not bad at all." How on earth (or after earth) can we cope successfully with a world to which we have blinded ourselves?

What would this hell look like? Swedenborg was not careful to sort out his descriptions by level, but we can at least speculate; and the following represents a fairly free embellishment of some of the images he offers. In its own light, the dominant feature of the behavioral hell would presumably be strength. The houses would be rugged, with shuttered windows and heavy doors. They would face away from each other, and there would be an abundance of massive stone walls around individual properties. I suspect that the prevailing egomania would make my own home look like a castle— more Norman than rococo in style, certainly. The landscape would have only the beauty of aridity. It would look massive and majestic. There would be no tender herbs, no soft contours, nothing in the least impractical. The people would be tall, muscular, and alert, and as heavily armed as they could manage.

In heaven's light, all of this strength would look like the pretense that it actually is. The houses would be small, cramped, and lightless, crowding in on each other. The air would be smoky with smoldering resentments, the people hunched and wary, the voices strident. There would be no sense of order, no city plan. There would certainly be many houses lying in ruins, casualties of the latest insurrection. There would be efforts at rebuilding, efforts hampered by the fact that everyone of us was trying to do as little as possible and get the most possible work out of everyone else. It would have to be terribly noisy, because, as the old ministerial joke has it, when the point we are trying to make is weak, we yell like hell. There would be no beauty to the aridity of the landscape—it would be simply bleak, colorless, and harsh.

I should perhaps highlight one assumption in all this that might otherwise slip by unnoticed, namely, that we are not talking about some kind of "steady-state" hell. There is none of the relentless broiling of the traditional caricature. We are talking about a life that has its ups and downs, its times of exultation as well as its times of depression, its pleasures as well as its pains. This strikes me as eminently realistic. After all, if evil were nothing but unrelieved pain, it would not be long before we were all very good indeed and hating every minute of it. No, once again, Swedenborg's hell takes very seriously the fact that we are capable of enjoying hatred and violence. Which capture our imagination—Milton's angels or his Satan?

The SECOND HELL, the one that focuses on intellect, would be far more sophisticated. Here we are wrapped up in the conviction of our own brilliance, and that conviction shapes the world around us. Seen in its

own light, its centers would be its universities and research labs, its concert halls and museums. It would have
immense libraries, brilliant salons, coffee houses where
adventurous minds stimulated each other. The presses
would be rolling night and day, fueled by the lively competitive spirit of gifted and ambitions writers. The center of each house would be the study, a space set apart
from the intense exchanges of the public forum, a private space where our deepest thoughts could take form,
could mature.

As the architecture of the behavioral hell focused
on strength, our architecture here would focus on the
use of light and would use it with impressive ingenuity.
Light would be used to delight and divert, to highlight
the unexpected, to surprise and even to bewilder. Every
new use of light would suggest further innovations,
spurring a constant creativity and creating a kind of instant obsolescence. There would certainly be a rich and
flourishing artistic life as well, with galleries constantly
supplied with new creations, concerts of dazzling and
original music, drama of literate grace and power.

In heaven's light, all this would be shadowy and de-
ceptive—everything would be smoke and mirrors. The
libraries would be dusty, the books unread, for the simple reason that if we already know it all, there is no
sense wasting time reading the infantile productions of
the ignorant. All the dazzle would be faint and flicker-
ing, all the ingenuity would be mere illusion. The brilliant salons would be cacophonies in which everyone
talked at once and no one really listened, in which the
goal was simply victory in the debate. An incident
in Jesus's life comes to mind in which he answered

questioners by asking them whether John's baptism was from heaven or not.[2] This posed an insoluble dilemma, it seems, because if they said it was from heaven he could ask why they had not believed in it, while if they answered that it was of strictly human origin, they would run afoul of the strong current of public opinion. John had come to be revered as a true prophet.

What is totally and spectacularly missing in this calculation is any concern for whether John's baptism actually was from heaven or not. Whether the answer was true or not simply did not matter. What mattered was the effect either answer might have on their own prestige. So in the salons and coffee houses of this hell, we are constantly maneuvering for position, for advantage. We are constantly seeking disciples, people who will look up to us. We are also constantly looking for rising stars to whom we can attach ourselves, trying to judge the currents of popular thought and ride them to prominence.

What are some of the sins of the mind? The scholarly world can be a violent one in its own way. One of my favorite professors retired early from a very promising career because he could no longer stomach academic politics. I gather that one of my most gifted and gentle classmates fell prey to the same forces.

What is going on here? I would suggest that we are looking at struggles for power, with the currency being jealously guarded intellectual property. Realistically, I find it impossible to distinguish exactly what in my thought and writing is "mine" and what comes from others. Everything seems to be in some measure both.

---

2. Matthew 21:23–27, Mark 11:27–23, Luke 20:1–8.

Yet the academic world has developed stringent rules for the claiming and defense of intellectual "property," and scholars sometimes seem to have no hesitation about destroying each other for violations of these rules. Under the highly civilized, even ritualized, surface, battles for tenure can be internecine, with every publication designed to be impregnable to attack, no stance taken that cannot be defended to the death.

One of the most effective tools in this game is the specialized language of the field. This is the membership card, so to speak. If we cannot manipulate the technical language of the field, we are not allowed into the game. Granted that it may be an efficient means of communication among specialists, mastering it does not guarantee insight.

Perhaps I am particularly sensitive on this score because I experience it as one of the constant threats to the integrity of my own church. Swedenborgianism has its distinctive and hallowed terminology—*conjugial* might head the list, with *discrete degrees; natural, spiritual, and celestial; influx; will and understanding; regeneration* and a host of others in hot pursuit. As I read much of our literature, I am not impressed with our skill in detecting congenial thought when it is couched in unfamiliar terms or, for that matter, in detecting uncongenial thought when it is dressed in familiar clothing. If you can use this language with some accuracy, then you are "one of us." If you cannot, then you are asking us to do the really hard work of trying to understand what it is you are trying to say. Extract the essence of this attitude, distill it, if you will, and you have minds that prize words over meanings, sounds over thoughts, the facade over the substance.

In the religious world in general, this is the hell of rigid and unforgiving orthodoxy. Sometimes it seems as though the Christian doctrine of the trinity was deliberately designed to make it impossible to say anything that was absolutely proof against the accusation of heresy. Certainly it was used time and again as a weapon in struggles for power. Certainly, too, Christianity is not the only major religion with a history of intolerance. It just happens to be my religion, which affords me the freedom of criticizing it.

On another front, the world of the arts is rarely as lovely under the surface as is the public face it presents, as witness the personal tragedies that hit the headlines from time to time. Agents make fortunes out of the fact that a lot of hornblowing is called for, and it is counterproductive for us to do too much of it ourselves. We therefore acquiesce in a kind of fiction and hire someone to say the things about us that would sound conceited if we were caught saying them. "Pay no attention to that man behind the curtain"—just keep looking at the larger-than-lifesize image he is presenting.

So, in the second hell, our brilliant books, our daring compositions, our stirring dramas turn out to be "same old same old" rewrites, star vehicles with ourselves as the star. "Underneath all the tinsel and glitter, there's *real* tinsel and glitter." Our intellects are wholly occupied not with the effort to understand things as they are, but to create the illusion that they are as we want them to be. From any practical point of view, this makes no sense whatever. It is like trying to create the illusion that there is plenty of gas in the tank when it is nearly empty, or perhaps more compellingly, like trying to convince ourselves that the strange lump in the breast or the abdomen isn't really there.

Under the surface brilliance of this intellectual hell, under the ingenuity and charm, there is an appalling stupidity. Intelligent people keep learning; but, in this hell, actual learning is the very last thing we want to do. It might contradict the beliefs we have invested ourselves in. The "no retreat" of the scholar can lead to an absolute dead end. The determination to be one up can lead to a lifelong devotion to discovering even the slightest faults in the work of our rivals and a total blindness to any merits such work may have.

What does all this look like in heaven's light? We are abysmally nearsighted, our voices are shrill and repetitive, and our posture is distinctly arachnid. The walls of our homes are hung with self-portraits. Our studies are dark dens where we lick our intellectual wounds and plot our counterattacks. We are alternately ingratiating and snide, utterly convinced of our own brilliance and prepared to acknowledge the reflected glory of anyone who seems to share that conviction. And again, we are surrounded by people like ourselves. There is no one, absolutely no one, we can trust, no one who understands, no one who cares in the least about us. We matter supremely to ourselves, and not at all to anyone else.

It may be appropriate at this point to bring in something that Swedenborg states with complete confidence, but which for me lies beyond the kind of empirical corroboration that I find for most of his statements about the other world. It is the statement that the Lord's providence is constantly active in all the hells to make sure that the violence and cruelty are kept within bounds. No matter how hard they try, no matter how skilful or vicious they are, evil spirits cannot succeed in their goal of destroying each other. This could mean that our very indestructability would stand as a constant reminder of our supreme worth.

In this world, sometimes it seems that there is no limit to the spiritual harm we can inflict on each other. People can be terribly traumatized, traumatized beyond our ability to heal. I can only trust that there is a kind of shut-down mechanism that kicks in when one's core being is actually threatened, that there is a kind of inner citadel to which we can retreat, so fortified that even the strongest signals from the outside cannot get through. My faith in God's justice is not threatened by a belief that we are capable of choosing hell forever. It is threatened by the thought that someone else could send us there against our will.[3]

Swedenborg associates the THIRD HELL particularly with the malignant creation of illusions; for me, this works like a charm. Our feelings, undisciplined by rationality or any realism, construct fantastic worlds where anything can happen. This, in its own light, is a world of epics on a cosmic scale, a world in constant transformation, shot through with sound and color, dramatic in the extreme. We may be Michael confronting the dragon or St. Patrick ridding the land of poisonous snakes or Ponce de Leon discovering the fountain of youth or Joan of Arc defending the faith or a rock idol

---

3. Perhaps the nearest thing to replication in our own experience would be Victor Frankl's discovery of faith and love in the death camps of the Holocaust. A kind of divine protection would explain the spiritual and psychological survival of individuals so appallingly assaulted.

with the world at our feet or Wanda Landowska redefin-
ing the harpsichord—it's our world. We are creating it
moment by moment, and as our whims change, our
world changes.

Visually, I think of the various worlds of science fiction, of mythic lands or stunning cloudscapes. This is a
lush world where everything is warm and alive. There is
nothing arid or angular here. Beanstalks grow to the sky
overnight, and the yellow brick road leads to the Emer-
ald City. In short, it is a world where wishes come true.

Of course, it's not quite that simple because we are
not alone. Everyone else in our world is a creator as
well, which means that there are cosmic conflicts, vast,
sky-sweeping battles in which the odds are against us.
Occasionally, we may prevail, and our illusions may in-
vade the minds of our opponents; but more often we
find ourselves to be the martyrs. The silver lining to this
cloud is that no one envies the winner's lot. Defeat renders us relatively inconspicuous. It is victory that ex-
poses us. It is the throne that has a target painted on it.

Heaven's light discloses why the conflicts are on
such a cosmic scale, and it is really fairly obvious. Our
cosmos is minute. We have shrunk reality down to our
own size because that is the only way we can be the gi-
ants we believe we are. To turn to the world of our
everyday lives, it does not take much trouble to fill our
horizons if our horizons are cramped enough. In
heaven's light, the warmth is fetid, and the lushness is
that of a swamp. We ourselves are images of our own
unique blends of self-gratification and rage, the sorts of
creature one expects to find under a rock. This is the

ultimate regression, the rejection of virtually everything that might make us truly human.

There is, in fact, something infantile about this hell. Psychologists speak of the infantile sense of omnipotence, the feeling that everything that happens is happening in response to us. It is the feeling that makes us hesitate to watch our favorite team because every time we do, they lose. It is also the mentality that is so totally absorbed in the present that misery is total misery and joy is total joy. There is no capacity to step outside and gain a sense of proportion.

It is one thing, though, to experience life this way in infancy, before we have differentiated ourselves from what we will come to regard as the outside world. It is quite another thing to have reinforced this attitude by a lifelong practice of fending off every challenge to it. To do this requires the deliberate demeaning of everyone who stands in our way, and that ultimately includes everyone whom we perceive as claiming a measure of recognition—meaning everyone in our world. Under the surface in this world, out in the open in the world to come, there is an utter contempt for anyone but ourselves, a contempt that flares up as vicious hatred whenever there is an actual challenge to our sole deity. After all, we cannot control what someone else creates, so we must be the sole creator.

This, I would suggest, is the mentality of the fanatic. Loyalty to a cause can provide a cloak of invisibility for it. In the name of country, race, or church, we can cast a halo of righteousness on the most barbaric of cruelties—witness the Oklahoma City bombings or the mutilations in Angola or the Inquisition or the Salem witch trials. The people who did these things did them not for themselves but "for the cause," utterly blind to their bestial brutality, utterly blind to their own supreme egotism. As long as we are content to pretend that there is a kind of nobility to chauvinism, we will be vulnerable to such tragedies. As long as we believe that our own cause justifies callousness, we will participate in the spiritual climate that breeds such violent storms. As long as we blind ourselves to the way the cause, however noble in theory, can serve as a cloak for self-deification, the door is not only unlocked, it is wide open.

Events that hit the headlines—events in Oklahoma City or Angola—provide publicly accessible images, but they may mislead us. They are the big events, and we may wind up assuming that the little events of our own lives are not all that important. I find Swedenborg warning us not to be so preoccupied with quantity that we overlook the decisive nature of quality. Hard science, true, has made enormous strides by limiting itself to what can be quantified, but there is more to our lives than "how much." When Kuwait was invaded, many people in my age bracket were taken back to the 1930s, when, on the far side of the ocean, a nobody named Hitler invaded the minor neighboring country of Czechoslovakia. This was not worth going to war about, not because it was qualitatively excusable but because it was quantitatively unimpressive. It turned out that the quality was the true harbinger of things to come. It turned out that the quality very shortly bred the quantity.

I mention this because it illustrates a fundamental principle of Swedenborg's hell. It is simply the ultimate

extension of the worst in us. It is what our own self-gratification, our own self-inflation, inevitably leads to if
given free rein. We deceive ourselves by cloaking such
attitudes with social graces, with sexual charm, with eru-
dition, or with piety, by setting them to stirring martial
music, by giving them the dramatic lines of heroism.
They are no less venomous on the personal scale than
they are on the wide screen.

Television shows us the large-scale events, but few
of us participate actively in them. For most of us, life focuses day after day on "the trivial round, the common
task." The scary people M. Scott Peck describes in *People of the Lie* are not major figures on the world scene.
Their victims are not whole ethnic minorities or buildings full of government workers. Their victims are a single son, a single husband; and in some ways the pain is
all the more deeply felt because it is not hidden in a
blaze of statistics. We can identify with that single son
because his, like ours, is a single story. We can identify
with that individual husband because we can follow the
workings of his mind for a while.

I call attention to this to underscore the significance of our own little lives. It may be quite true that
there is not much we can do about the state of the
world, but we can hardly overestimate how important
we are to each other. The feelings that Peck's victims
arouse in us are reminders of the infinite worth of every
individual soul. In downsizing the "cosmic" battles of
the third hell, I spoke of our self-deification as shrinking
the cosmos down to our own minute size, but it would
be more accurate to say that the soul has no fixed size. If
we let the cosmos in, the soul expands. If we shut it out,

it shrinks. If we let others into our hearts, they have room to grow. If we shut them out, we shut ourselves in. There is nothing inherently "small" about our individual lives. Their effective size is up to us.

In short, Swedenborg does not offer us a choice between spirituality and social responsibility. There is nothing exclusively private about his spirituality. His heaven and his hell are societal, and are both active and mirrored in our present human communities. Again and again we are reminded that "the other world" is as close to us as our own thoughts and feelings. It is the realm of our unseen motivations. It is the geography of our own relationships, the space in which we move closer to each other in mutual understanding and affection or farther from each other in mutual misunderstanding and suspicion, regardless of our location in this physical world.

The highest usefulness of Swedenborg's pictures of hell is not to terrify us with fears about the future but to alert us to threats to our souls in the present. What does our egocentricity look like when the masks are stripped off? Are we the handsome, dramatic devils of *Paradise Lost*, or are we small-minded, venomous, deformed creatures who flee from the light lest our actual bestiality be exposed to view? There is really no point in deceiving ourselves.

eight

wHat aBout tHe BiBLe?

Not long ago, Pope John Paul issued a description or definition of hell as essentially a state of alienation from God. According to one newspaper account, there were immediate objections from literalist Christians who insisted that the Bible taught that hell was a physical place of physical torment, a location where the unredeemed suffered in real, eternal flames. It should not be reduced to something merely psychological. By now it should be clear that I am much more in agreement with the pope than with the literalists and that, in this regard as in others, I follow Swedenborg.

I will be looking at the biblical witness in this chapter. It is clearly the primary source of the images of heaven and hell that permeate our Western culture. The Bible more than any other work has informed our art and our literature. When a secular culture rejects notions of heaven and hell, it is biblical images that are at issue.

To lay some foundation for a look at the biblical witness, I would first of all urge that there is nothing trivial about psychological pain. Spirit is solid and powerful stuff. People have committed suicide in perfect health, free of physical pain, because they were in mental torment. It may have been a sense of guilt or of shame, it may have been an overpowering sense of hopelessness or worthlessness—the main point is simply that pain does not have to be physical to be real. I do not find it necessary to believe in physical hellfire to believe in a very real hell.

Still, to restrict the torment of hell to an inner awareness of alienation from God is to ignore the societal dimension of our lives. There are two "great commandments," not one, and I believe the message is that they are inseparable. To paraphrase the first epistle of John, if I cannot love the neighbor I can see, how can I love a God whom I cannot see (1 John 4:20)? Hell is not just how I feel about myself. It is also how I perceive and treat you because of those feelings and how you perceive and treat me.

I do have some genuine sympathy for literalists. People have been reached by the graphic image of eternal fire who probably could not be reached in any other way, and I would be false to my own faith if I denied or belittled this. A few years ago, I found myself standing next to a flight attendant while waiting for the door to open for deplaning. We got talking, and when she discovered that I was a minister, she became a different person. The professionally cheerful and efficient uniform was replaced by sheer joy. She had recently been born again, and she was radiant, quite lovely. I strongly suspect that we would have disagreed about the nature of eternal damnation—most born-again experiences are set in a literalist context—but that was quite beside the point.

I would also be false to my own faith, though, if I ignored the fact that other people, people of equal value in the Lord's sight, have been turned away by a picture that they cannot reconcile with their belief in a loving God. They cannot respect the injustice of a God who would accept the sacrifice of a devoted son to deliver people from punishment that, presumably, they thoroughly deserved. Many bear scars of childhood terror, convinced that what has been imposed on them was the will of God when, in fact, it was the will of the church or of their parents. Others find the scriptural portrayals of hell—or, at least, the popular images that have arisen from them—simplistic; and, as already noted, very thoughtful Christians have found it impossible to reconcile these pictures with the notion of a God who is both good and omnipotent.

It needs first to be observed that the literalist is talking more from Scripture than from reason or experience, and one thing that is at issue here is not simply the authority of Scripture but its nature as well. That is my focus in this chapter, and it is a huge topic. For me, claims to the authority of Scripture are most often smoke screens for claims of the authority of the church or of some particular reading of Scripture. Genuine authority, I would argue, is an intrinsic quality of reality. When things become real to us, we pay attention to them. Most of the arguments for the authority of Scripture feel more like efforts to invest with authority something that has not become real, a least to the people on the receiving end of the argument. The time spent in such argument might better be spent in trying to make vivid what the Bible is saying.

This is no simple matter. Among the millions of people who have accepted the Bible as divine revelation down through the centuries, there has been an immense variety of readings, some attempting to be rigorously literal, others highly imaginative.[1] Currently, we find in the academic world approaches labeled as historical, sociological, narrative, feminist, liberation, and canonical, among others. Further, while it is all very well to insist that Scripture is to be taken literally, the fact is that literalists do not agree with each other. There is no single fundamentalist denomination comprising all the people who see clearly what the Bible teaches. Far from it, literalist churches have been just as prone to schism as liberal ones, and the schisms have often been bitter. To glimpse the problem faced by literalists (or created by literalism?), we need only look at Paul asserting that we are justified by faith apart from the works of the law (Romans 3:28), and then look at James asserting that we are justified by our works and not by faith alone (James

---

1. I am indebted to the Reverend Dr. Jonathan Rose for calling my attention to Jesus's *two* questions in Luke 10: 26: first, "What is written in the law?" and then, "How do you read it?"

2:24). You pays your money and takes your choice. Before Paul makes the case for salvation by faith, he has already described God as one who will reward people according to their works, giving "glory, honor and peace to everyone who does good: first for the Jew, then for the Greek" (Romans 2:10), but I am not aware of any conservative Christian church, or any liberal one, for that matter, that teaches that Jews are the first to be rewarded. Still, "That's what the Bible says," plain and simple.

Biblical literalism as we know it is, I believe, a relative newcomer on the scene. It may claim an apostolic pedigree, but only on a very simplistic reading of history. It has a strong polemical cast, the enemy being secular interpretations of reality, and there was no such enemy in apostolic times. Until the development of scientific inquiry in the Enlightenment, there was no particular reason to doubt the biblical accounts of creation and the history that followed them. There was every reason to believe, because these accounts gave meaning to everyday life.[2] They gave people a sense of *why* our world came into being, a sense of the purpose of it all. They offered this sense of purpose, and this was assumed to be their primary intent.

Then science came along asking *how* the world was created and started coming up with some answers very different from the ones people were used to. Science, however, was asking a different question. I was surprised some years ago to discover that Darwin

---

2. See Brevard Childs, "The *Sensus Literalis* of Scripture: An Ancient and Modern Problem" in *Beiträge zur alttestamentlichen Theologie*, eds. Herbert Donner, Robert Hanhart, and Rudolf Smend (Göttingen: Vandenhoek & Ruprecht, 1977).

explicitly denied being the originator of the idea of evolution. In *The Origin of Species*, he refers to a French botanist named Naudin who believed "that species are formed in an analogous matter as varieties are under cultivation"; but Darwin objects that "he does not show how selection acts under nature. He believes, like Dean Herbert, that species, when nascent, were more plastic than at present. He lays weight on what he calls the principle of finality, (and here I translate from Naudin's French), 'a mysterious, undefined power called fatalism by some and a providential will by others . . . .'"[3] In his footnote to this section, Darwin mentions that Naudin is one of thirty four-authors "who believe in the modification of species." Darwin saw his contribution as the identification of the *mechanism* behind this modification. To act "under nature" is to act independently of any "principle of finality" or purpose, independently of any "providential will." It is to rule out the "why" question.

Logically, there was nothing necessarily atheistic about his proposal. Why and how are separable questions. You may be able to explain how Roger Bannister managed to break the four-minute barrier, drawing on detailed knowledge of human physiology,[4] but that will not bring you closer to understanding why he did it, an interesting question in its own right. It required a remarkable level of motivation as well as remarkable

---

3. Charles Darwin, *The Origin of the Species* (New York: Knopf, Modern Editions, year), 8.

4. I learned in 1994 that the breakthrough in training came after he and his colleagues, Christopher Chataway and Christopher Brasher, took a weekend off for mountain climbing—a kind of unintentional high-altitude training.

physical gifts. In his quest to understand the "mechanism" (a carefully chosen word, surely), Darwin consciously, deliberately, we might even say *purposefully*, ruled out the question of purpose; and this is a very different thing from demonstrating that there is no purpose. Far from it, by ruling out the question, he disqualified himself from offering an answer to it, either affirmative or negative.

Perhaps some of the difficulty rests in the fact that we use the words "why" and "because" in relation to both past causes and future purposes. I buy a scanner *because* I want to be able to send pictures to my children on-line at some future time, and the scanner is available to me *because* of a whole series of past events. Have we come to think that there is only one "why," that the power we have gained by learning about past causes somehow erases the future ones, or shows them to be illusory? If it can be shown that my values are rooted in my history, does that show that I do not look ahead?

The "why" questions will not go away. They are the stuff of religion. In the October 1991 issue of *The National Geographic Magazine*, Alfonso Ortiz wrote eloquently about the function of Tewa myths:

> I too have been to Soviet Asia and seen cave art and an old ceremonial costume remarkably similar to some found in America. But a Tewa is not so interested in the work of archaeologists. A Tewa is interested in our own story of our origin, for it holds all that we need to know about our people, and how one should live as a human. The story defines our society. It tells me who I am, where I came

from, the boundaries of my world, what kind of order exists within it; how suffering, evil, and death came into this world; and what is likely to happen to *me* when I die.[5]

Again, the archeologist's explanations of how do not satisfy the longing to understand why, the need to know.

Frankly, whether the world was created in six days or in billions of years does not matter much to me. The technology associated with the scientific answer has, of course, enabled me to be much more efficient in what I do, but the Big Bang hypothesis itself does not affect the way I treat my wife and children or the value I attach to my students. It does not affect my spending priorities or my driving habits. However, when I read that the human race has been given dominion over the fish of the sea and the fowl of the air (Genesis 1:26), I am confronted with an inescapable responsibility. I am being told "who I am," a member, whether I like it or not, of the most powerful class of creatures on earth. I am being told "what kind of order exists" in my world—that my position is not to be taken lightly. This awareness does affect the way I treat my wife and children, the value I attach to my students, my spending priorities, and my driving habits. It denies me the luxury of heedless self-indulgence; it impels me to look at the effects of my decisions.

It impels me all the more as technology amplifies my effectiveness. In the backyard of our house in

---

5. Alfonso Ortiz, "Through Tewa Eyes: Origins," *National Geographic Magazine* 180, no. 4 (October 1991).

Massachusetts, there was a shallow stone-lined pit where previous residents had discarded their trash. In an era before packaging dwarfed contents, in an era when nothing that could be reused would be discarded, this did no great harm. With the energy we now have at our disposal, with the mechanization that has made replacement cheaper than repair, the effects of this practice would be ruinous. For another example, no matter how recklessly I run, I am not likely to hurt anyone but myself very seriously if I lose control. But put me behind the wheel of a ton or more of vehicle, and the effects of losing control are likely to be extensive and fatal. Far from rendering questions of purpose and meaning irrelevant, technology has made them more urgent than ever.

The Bible, I would urge, does not much care about the "how" questions. It is intensely concerned with the "whys." It makes only passing reference to the fact that the Philistines had an immense technological edge over the Israelites, having mastered the smelting of iron (1 Samuel 13:19–21). As far as the story is concerned, the outcome of the struggle for the Promised Land hinged on God's purpose and Israel's faith. The prophets paid little attention to the economic and military insignificance of Israel or Judah in comparison with the might of Assyria or Babylon. As far as they were concerned, national survival depended on ethical integrity, on the keeping of covenant. The whole drama is impelled by God's purposes, and time and again the hearer is reminded not to trust weapons or horses or numbers.

Beyond this, careful scholarly research makes it abundantly clear that, in biblical times, it was taken for granted that there would be hidden meanings in any sacred text. We need not turn to academic journals for evidence of this. The Gospel of Matthew, with its attention to the theme of the fulfillment of prophecy, offers a rich sampling of the principles of Scripture interpretation that obtained in the early days of the Christian church. For example, seen in its own literal context, the prophecy associated with the virgin birth proves to point in quite a different direction. It speaks not of a virgin (*bethulah*) but of a maiden (*'almanah*), and it is clearly talking about a child to be born in the near future, during the reign of Hezekiah (Isaiah 7:14, Matthew 1:23).[6] When John the Baptist identifies himself as the "voice crying in the wilderness," he is referring to a prophecy that God would descend and change the whole landscape, raising valleys and leveling mountains (Isaiah 40:3, Matthew 3:3), which Matthew's readers knew perfectly well had not happened. The prophecy "out of Egypt have I called my son" is not a prophecy at all, but part of a narration of the gracious acts of God in the past (Matthew 2:15, Hosea 11:1). Perhaps most spectacularly, when John the Baptist is identified as the Elijah who is to come, he is identified as the herald of the day that will "burn like a furnace," when the wicked will be consumed like stubble (Malachi 4:1, 5, Matthew 11:14). And perhaps most "illiteral," the prophecy "He shall be called a Nazarene," a person from Nazareth, can refer only to the prophecy "He [Samson!] shall be a Nazar*ite*," a kind of ascetic (Judges 13:5,7; Matthew

---

6. Matthew's reading of the prophecy was doubtless facilitated by the fact that the Jewish Greek translation of the Hebrew Bible, the Septuagint, rendered `almanah` as *parthenos*, which has strong connotations of chastity.

2:23). Any literalist of the modern stripe would have dismissed Matthew in a moment. Instead, no attention whatever is paid to the fact that the prophecies cited by Matthew were *not* fulfilled literally. Mountains were not leveled, and the wicked were not burned like stubble.

Matthew knew his audience. He was a man of his times, not of ours. He knew that the divine voice was oracular. God did not speak in the prosaic language of mere mortals but in words freighted with hidden meaning. Only a simpleton would take them at face value. The power of his citations lay in the "Aha!" experience of having one of these hidden meanings brought out into the light, illuminating both the text and the current event that was fulfilling it. It was like having the piece or the letter added to the puzzle that suddenly made clear both the "meaning" of the individual piece and the overall pattern, that resolved a confusion of unrelated bits into the beginnings of coherence.

So if someone had confronted Matthew with his cavalier attitude toward the letter, if someone had charged him with being fanciful, he would probably have been bewildered. Why would anyone care about Hezekiah's understanding of an ancient prophecy when the world was being changed before their very eyes? Why would anyone quibble about anything as pedestrian as the tenses of verbs? Could anyone be so naive, or so arrogant, as to believe that the whole mind of God could be contained in the most prosaic of interpretations? Was there no mystery at all to the Divine? The legends of the time were full of stories of people who had taken the utterances of oracles literally and who had met disaster as a result.

This whole mental world was very different from that of the Enlightenment. I would argue that the both the church and science failed to see how things had changed and how they were asking different questions. Not only that, science, encouraged by triumph after triumph, began more and more to assume that what it could not (or would not) study was not worth studying or did not even exist. The church began more and more to insist that its answers to the why questions were divinely revealed answers to the how questions. Perhaps without realizing it, it joined science in the assumption that the physical world was of supreme importance. The stage was set for polarization, with each side defending itself by attacking the other and with every attack prompting a more determined defense. Science became more and more resolutely irreligious, while the church became more and more resolutely dogmatic, and both agreed that the battle was to be fought on the field of materialism.

This polarization was particularly acute in relation to those books and passages of Scripture classed as "apocalyptic," the descriptions of cosmic events that are to take place at the close of the age or at the end of time. It takes very little knowledge of astronomy to realize that a star is not going to fall on the earth (Revelation 9:10). The falling would be in the other direction, since the gravitational pull of even the smallest star would dwarf that of our little planet. If we discount that, we must still explain how most of the earth survives this collision, how it is that in succeeding verses and chapters we still read of people and places, of grass and locusts, of land and sea. And let us admit no argument that these "stars" are really only meteors. If I know the difference between a star and a meteor, surely their Creator, the omniscient author of Scripture, does.

The level on which these passages can be accepted as true is quite different. It is evidenced by the power with which they have addressed and evoked human fears and longings over the centuries. The last trumpet, the four horsemen, and the grim reaper have caught and held our attention. The Book of Revelation presents graphic images of an omnipotent deity, of the fury of evil, of the clash between the two, and the inevitable victory of true divinity. To borrow from Jungian thought, they speak in the potent and evocative language of archetypes. For souls caught in a harsh, chaotic world, they are a beacon of hope, a well of courage. This is a *big* God, and all the apparently awesome might of this unjust world is really only sound and fury, signifying nothing.

Nowadays we have highly developed philosophical and theological languages for conveying this message in abstract terms. We have a mistrust of imagery because, by comparison with the languges of science or even of formal theology, it seems undisciplined. It makes suggestions, it invites the mind to imagine and seems to exert little control over the imagination that it has let loose. Yet, I would insist, the Bible is an imaginative book. There are very few "abstract" terms in biblical Hebrew; and while Greek had developed a philosophical vocabulary by the time of Christ, the Gospels make little use of it. Jesus told stories, used imagery. For him, the concrete was the vessel of the intangible. He did not define "the neighbor" but told a story of a man who fell among thieves. He did not write an essay on justice but told stories about stewards and landlords. He did not draw up a job description for the Messiah but talked about sheep and shepherds. In good Eastern fashion, he paid his disciples the profound compliment of provoking their minds rather than satisfying them. He turned them loose to figure things out for themselves. If literalists were as literal about pastoral responsibility as they are about hellfire, there would be a lot more people out on the hills with their sheep than there actually are. We would be big into vineyards and olive groves, lamps on lampstands, and cups of cold water. There would surely be some who had cut off an offending hand or plucked out an offending eye.

As I reflect on all this, a kind of principle begins to emerge, namely, that, as long as spirit seems unreal or insubstantial, the material reigns supreme, as in fact it must. We need something to hold on to, and it must feel solid. Paul tried hard to get this message across with his insistence on the resurrection of the body. In the resurrection, we would not be disembodied thoughts or diaphanous shades; we would be substantial people. He tried to make it clear that this was a spiritual rather than a material substantiality; but to the materialist, that is an intolerable oxymoron (See 1 Corinthians 15:44). I would refer again to the testimony of NDEers that one of the most important things they learned was that they are spiritual beings *here and now*. Their own spirits have become real to them, real and utterly important.

This means that malice, for example, is solid stuff. It is far easier for me to control my physical behavior than to control my tastes, my feelings. Until we become vividly aware of the consuming, substantive destructiveness of exclusive self-concern, of the enduring rage inherent in self-deification, the Swedenborgian hell must seem indefensibly mild. In fact, Swedenborg is saying, hell's "fire" is unquenchable by its very nature. There is simply no way in this world or the next that it can be satisfied. To borrow from Greek mythology, we need only posit that it is Sisyphus' own ambition to put the rock on top of the mountain. He is totally unwilling to recognize that it has its own proper place at the bottom. That is where it wants to be; and, if he would only leave it there, he might find something much more rewarding to do. All his suffering is rooted in his craving for what cannot be.

Once we awaken to the import, the sheer power, of the inner world, the language of imagery is irresistible. We see our hopes and fears reflected in light and darkness, in storm and calm, in fire and flame, in depth and height. We see our peculiar qualities of heart and mind reflected in animals ("Go tell that fox . . ." [Luke 13:32]), our changing moods in the seasons ("The harvest is abundant, . . ." [Matthew 9:37]), our inner struggles in physical conflicts ("Every kingdom divided against itself . . ." [Luke 11:17]). The invisible world, the world of purpose and meaning, is mirrored in the visible, rendered communicable; and one result of this is a change in our relationship to the visible world. It is no longer an end in itself. It has the added value of translucence.

I have already offered the thought that we can project curves for our physical and our mental/spiritual stories and that these curves may and often do diverge in our later years. To this I would add the thought that this divergence urges us to take the inner side of things more seriously. The physical world does become less vivid and harder to deal with, less and less rewarding, as we grow older. It is as though a door were being gradually closed. Helen Keller believed that, whenever one door of happiness was closed to us (and she had more than her share of closed doors), another opened. She urged us not to stare so fixedly at the closed door that we fail to see the opening one.[7]

In other words, I would see the aging process itself as nudging us away from materialism and its attendant literalism, prompting us to reflect on what really matters to us. We may look to Scripture in this regard. The Bible tells how Israel labored and fought for the establishment of an earthly kingdom, how it actually found success under David—and how that kingdom failed. It tells us that, even in the midst of that failure, hope did not die; and in the prophets and the Gospels, it tells of a reponse to that hope, but a response with a twist. The new convenant is not like the old. The new covenant is not written on stone tablets but on the heart (Jeremiah 31:31). We find Jesus, like John the Baptist, proclaiming not the kingdom of Israel but the kingdom of heaven. We find the prophecies being fulfilled in unexpected ways, on another, nonliteral level.

The Gospels are deeply rooted in the Hebrew Bible. When Matthew outlines the fourteen-generation spans between Abraham and David, David and the exile, and the exile and the Messiah, he is telling his audience something it needs to know. Abraham, David, and the exile have been the great turning points in the story.

---

7. *The Open Door*, op. cit., 11.

The Messiah is the present, an equally great turning point in that same story. Abraham is the promise of the earthly kingdom; David, the fulfullment of that promise; the exile, the failure of that fulfillment; and the Messiah, its transformation.

It will turn out that it is a turn upward or inward, a turn from the earthly to the spiritual. Yet it does not so much leave the earthly behind as transform it, "inspirit" it. There is nothing escapist about the spirituality of the Gospels. It is down-to-earth and earthy. It uses the language of earth as the embodiment of spirit in the language of parable. It uses, I would argue, the language of eternal fire as the embodiment of self-deification just as it uses the language of cosmic catastrophe to express the transcendent power of divinity.

In a sense, then, the spirituality of the Gospels claims to add nothing to the Scriptures in which it is rooted. Rather, it seeks to manifest what those Scriptures imply, to articulate what they take for granted. "Do not think that I have come to abolish the law or the prophets. I have not come to abolish but to fulfil" (Matthew 5:17). Jesus did not make up the two great commandments; he highlighted them—just as "a certain lawyer" did, with hostile intent (Luke 10:25–28). They are right there in the Torah, in Deuteronomy and Leviticus, plain as day.

That is, when the discovery of the reality of spirit renders the letter of Scripture translucent, the letter of Scripture is not diminished or rendered obsolete. Far from it, the text begins to speak with a depth appropriate to divinity. In the same way, when the discovery of the reality of spirit renders the material world translucent, the material world is not diminished or rendered obsolete. It actually takes on new value as it lends substantiality to the intangible, to the spirit. It provides invaluable means of communication.

Currently, for example, we seem to be paying a great deal of attention to something we call "stress." From a materialist point of view, real stress is a good Newtonian phenomenon. It can be observed and quantified. Its effects can be noted and recorded. It happens when a force is consistently or repeatedly applied to something that resists it, when something relatively passive is affected, especially over a span of time, by something relatively active.

Stress turns out to reflect the way we feel when circumstances keep threatening our own inner stability, when things are flowing in a way we cannot or do not want to go with. My favorite hypothetical example is of an employee who is told, "These are the results I want, and I won't ask any questions about how you get them." If the employee's ethical sensibility outweighs his or her ambition, this sets up a stressful situation. The demand presses against significant values, and something has to give. If the employee's ambitions outweigh his or her ethical sensibility, however, this represents a golden opportunity, a chance to get ahead of rivals who are more squeamish. There is no "something that resists," so there is no stress.

All this could probably be explained in the abstract language of academicians, but it wouldn't sell. Only the experts would understand, only the people who have spent the necessary years learning the language of the trade, the badge of membership in a particular scholarly elite. Whether or not there is really some "thing" within us that is resisting some "force" from the outside, the stress image communicates. It lends substance to the invisible. It brings it out from the strictly private realm of our inner selves into the light of shared experience, and it does so because physical stress is real and observable.

In fact, it may be that both the power and the sterility of materialistic science are evidenced by this kind of usage. It is from Newtonian physics that we have drawn some of our most familiar images of the unseen—not just stress but tension, friction, leverage, impact, action and reaction, pressure, inertia, and orbiting, to name a few. We wind up wincing when we see metal snapping under stress. I suspect it was a revelatory experience the first time someone actually spun the wheels of an automobile, something that does not happen with horse-drawn vehicles. What was it like to feel the application of power with absolutely no result? What thoughts did it evoke about human relationships? The mind turns away from "pure science" to such matters because they matter so much, and pure science ignores them.

To my mind, then, the hellfire of Scripture is trivialized by being taken merely literally. It is reduced to the opacity of matter, impervious to the spirit that gives our lives meaning. It becomes something that could be quantified, put on Bacon's rack and forced to yield its secrets to our technological appetites. Matter does matter, but not supremely. Our attention is caught by people who are physically attractive; but if we find them to be callous or manipulative, we feel that we have been deceived. The physical beauty should be a true representation of beauty of character. Since physical beauty does affect us, does make a difference, it is perhaps under-standable that we find ourselves feeling as though it is all that matters, but it is folly, nevertheless. I would argue that the insistence on physical hellfire is, ultimately, of the same order.

Again, I see nothing whatever wrong in being at-tracted by physical beauty. I see it, in fact, as an outward manifestation of a longing for the deeper qualities it suggests, which is why we feel deceived or even betrayed when those qualities are absent. Physical beauty is a most appropriate place to start because of what it can evoke. It is a most inappropriate place to stop because what it can evoke is what really matters. The whole ef-fort to preserve the appearances of youth, the immense and profitable industry that ranges from hair dyes to cosmetic surgery, runs the risk of trapping us in a world of pretense, a world of illusion. I would far rather have someone look at my homely and wrinkled face and see affection there than have them look at a handsome mask, a technological triumph over the effects of time, and not know what might lie behind it.

Even more disastrous than blindness to the spiritual is taking it to be unambiguously reflected in the physi-cal. One of the most difficult hours in my life was spent at the bedside of a woman who was dying of cancer. Her literalist faith told her two things: one, that the cancer must be a punishment for sin, and two, that it could therefore be cured by faith. Clearly, if she were to die of cancer it would be because her faith was inadequate. If she were to die of cancer, then, all she could expect was eternal damnation. Those who were with her were re-quired to pray for her healing with all the fervor we could muster because, in her mind and heart, that physical healing was inseparably wedded to her salvation. I could find no way through a wall of conviction that had been built by a lifetime of intense loyalty, no way to suggest that the cancer might not be a punishment, that she might die of cancer without being condemned to hell. As one of my colleagues remarked in response to a parishioner's profession of atheism, "Tell me about the god you don't believe in. I probably don't believe in that god either."

Let me summarize, then. The more convinced I become that the Bible is a divine revelation, is the Word of God, the more obvious it becomes that it has hidden depths of meaning. In fact, the more convinced I become that it has those hidden depths, the more obvious it is that it is a divine revelation. It represents a divine reaching down into our preoccupation with this transitory physical world to awaken us to the eternal world of the spirit. If it says things that are literally not true, that in itself may be a signpost that urges me to look deeper.

The Bible was not written by literalists, but by tellers of stories, people of spiritual substance who thought in concrete images. To literalize it is to deny its depths. It is to focus attention on the means of communication, on the typeface, so to speak, rather than on the message, on the face and the figure rather than on the character. Yes, this gives literalism the ability to get through to us when we are so preoccupied with physical concerns that spiritual ones seem illusory, and that is worth doing. But the very process of aging urges us to look deeper; and when we discover that the kingdom of heaven is indeed "at hand," while we may in a sense retain our affection for literalism's affirmations, we can no longer accept its denials.

Specifically, to insist on a literal, physical hellfire is ultimately to distract the mind from the inner hells we can choose here and now, the hells that give rise to everything from the physical abuse of children to the corporate greed that adulterates baby food in order to maximize profits, the hells that burned women at the stake a few centuries ago and that scream "God hates faggots" in our own times. The time comes in every life to lay the axe to the root of the tree, to move beyond a preoccupation with symptoms to an honest search for causes. It is when we engage in that search that the evocative language of the Bible comes into its own.

fRee foR aLL?

Lastly, I should like to touch on the theodicy question by looking at hell, heaven, and the here and now in respect to our freedom. Granted that it seems necessary to regard ourselves as free and responsible moral agents, it is obvious that our freedom is limited. We are not omnipotent. What is the nature of our freedom, and what are its limits? Here we immediately encounter what I take to be the central paradox of any serious thought about the human condition. I have already called attention to the paradox implicit in any claim that determinism is true. It may or may not be. If it is, we can only think that we know, because we believe whatever we have been conditioned to believe. No one escapes the laws of cause and effect.

Logically, religion is equally paradoxical. As soon as we posit an omnipotent God, there is no power left for us. As soon as we posit an infinite God, there is no room left for us. The closest thing I know of to a satisfactory handling of this dilemma is the concept of an infinite and omnipotent God who intends, who wills, our existence and our freedom, who intentionally empowers us, who is self-limiting for our sakes.[1] This is not a tight argument philosophically, but tight philosophical arguments usually have little to do with the values we build our lives around.

This leaves me with a kind of conditional existence, challenging the thought that I can claim any power as my own, undermining my instinctive assumptions of my own reality. I wind up with a revised version of Descartes' starting point, namely, *Videor cogitare, ergo videor esse*—I seem to think; therefore, I seem to exist. I am quite capable of looking into the mirror and wondering what it is that I am looking at, wondering how much of what I see is real and how much is illusion. My freedom seems to be just as real as I am, and I cannot ask for more. From a practical point of view, as already noted, our society depends on a tacit agreement that we are free moral agents and that it is, therefore, reasonable for us to hold each other accountable for our actions. We may from time to time plead the overwhelming pressure of circumstances, but there is a strong aversion to being put in situations where we "have no choice." It is only in the more rarefied realms

---

1. See Swedenborg's striking statement in *True Christian Religion* §33 that God began creation by "finiting his infinity."

of theory that strict determinism is a viable option. In practice, it makes life meaningless and societal living unworkable.

The limits to our freedom, however, are obvious. I cannot do just anything I feel like doing. There are limits to my physical strength, limits to my knowledge, limits to my intelligence, limits to my determination. From one point of view, I am really a very small person in a very big universe. I cannot understand most of the languages of our planet, do not know most of its inhabitants, have not read most of its books, have not seen most of its cities, and have not tasted most of its food; and there is no possible way that I can. In fact, I am obliged to select, to choose. As I noted in the first chapter, even in the little corner of the universe with which I am familiar, there is always too much for me to attend to, always more than I can take care of.

Even if strict determinism were in some fashion true, then, its actual usefulness, its practicality, would be limited. There are simply far too many influences on us. The fact that we can be awakened by a faint but unfamiliar sound testifies to the fact that we are taking in signals of which we are utterly unaware. I am focused on the computer screen; but, if a light were to shine on the window at the periphery of my vision, I would notice it. If I am receiving all these signals twenty-four hours a day, some consciously, more semiconsciously, and even more subconsciously, how can they be catalogued, and how can their total effect be calculated? How can my conditioning be analyzed, let alone adjusted to obtain desired results?

Further, the signals we receive are often not in

total agreement with each other. Whether it is two opportunities calling for the same stretch of time, two creditors claiming the same dollars, or two children, each demanding total attention, we regularly experience pulls and pushes in opposite directions. Here again, the fact that we are finite presents us with the necessity of choosing.

So much for the circumstantial dimension of freedom, the objective side, if you will. If it is granted that our circumstances, far from controlling our actions, conspire rather to send us multiple and often conflicting signals, that still says nothing about how we will respond. A choice that may paralyze one individual may energize another. The subjective dimension of freedom is of critical importance, and it is here that Swedenborg again focuses our attention. It is his categories that are reflected in the first sentence of this chapter in the reference to hell, heaven, and the here and now. He sees a particular kind of freedom as characteristic of each.

Let me take them in reverse order. Swedenborg describes us as being held, in the here and now, between calls to heaven and calls to hell, subject to pressures or, perhaps better, attractions, from both sides. He uses images of opposing forces so carefully balanced that the person at their intersection can tip the scales.[2] That is, freedom in the here and now is essentially a freedom to choose what kind of person we want to be. We may be spiritually as well as physically very small people in a very big universe, but an omnipotent and omnibenevolent providence makes sure that we are not

2. See, for example. *True Christian Religion* §478:2.

overwhelmed.[3] I think of this balance not as a static point, incidentally, but rather as a range in which the actual proportions are constantly shifting. It is just that there is a kind of governance that keeps those shifts within manageable limits.

My favorite image of this is the physics of walking or running. Someone (I have no idea who) described walking as a constant process of losing our balance and catching ourselves. That is, the balance of walking is a dynamic one, with a slight forward lean necessary if our feet are not to walk out from under us and leave us flat on our backs. Look at a photograph of the start of a hundred-meter dash, and check the angle of the runners' bodies. Watch a little one who is just learning to walk, or if you want to relive the difficulty the little one faces, try riding a unicycle.

This suggests a kind of instability inherent in spiritual freedom, an instability that is not necessarily welcome. It entails inner conflict that ranges all the way from mild discomfort to intense pain. It involves times when we do not like ourselves at all and times when we feel acutely that "the time is out of joint," as Hamlet says. We find ourselves having to say no to one thing we like in order to say yes to another, and sometimes it does not feel free at all. For generations, many women felt their freedom curtailed by their effective exclusion from

---

3. This is Paul's contention in 1 Corinthians 10:13. Swedenborg certainly recognizes that we may at times be swept away by our emotions (see, for example, *Marriage Love* §459), but evidently regards such occasions as exceptions. To rationalize or "confirm" such actions when the emotions are no longer in control is effectively to assume responsibility for them (*Arcana Coelestia* §9009).

the job market, while at the same time many men felt their freedom curtailed by the necessity of earning a living. It seems that we are not only free but that we often have no choice in the matter. We are forced into it by the fact that we cannot have everything we want or, more precisely, by the fact that we want mutually exclusive things.

Things begin to come clear for me when we turn to the other two freedoms, the heavenly and the hellish. At least in my reading of Swedenborg, the ambiguity of our feelings about having to choose are the natural result of our being in this intermediate position, being caught in this fundamental ambivalence. Part of us wants heavenly freedom and part of us wants hellish freedom, and here-and-now freedom is neither.

Heavenly and hellish freedom have one very important thing in common. Each is a freedom to be the kind of person we have chosen to be. Inner conflict is behind us. As a result of the sorting out that has taken place in the world of spirits, we are internally unanimous. In hell, we are not plagued by pangs of conscience or moments of doubt. We know the score. As angels, we spontaneously and wholeheartedly are warmed by each other's joys and delighted by each other's insights. We want to understand and be understood. We have nothing to hide, and live in a world that is free of pretense. Again, I would turn to the reports of the being of light before whom we are utterly transparent and by whom we are completely accepted.

It is hard for me to imagine a greater liberation than liberation from all need to keep up appearances, freedom simply to relax totally and be myself, with no inner voices raising doubts or asking embarrassing questions. There is nothing that I want to wall out. This is an absolute "being at home." It has the Taoist feel of being totally attuned to everything and everyone around us, of an environment that presents no obstacles because of that attunement. We move freely because the pattern, the design, that surrounds us is also within us. I think of the pianist who has truly mastered her art and who is marvelously free to express herself on the keyboard. The discipline has been internalized. It is no longer something imposed from without; it is part of her being, part of who she is.

Concert pianists are a few and far between, and this may seem like an unattainable goal for ordinary people. In fact, though, we regularly take for granted abilities that are equally miraculous. One of my favorite examples is the effortless ease with which we understand spoken language. The phonetic fact is that we are receiving an uninterrupted stream of incredibly complex sound waves—bewilderingly rapid and intricate changes in air pressure. Our eardrums are vibrating, little bones in our ears are rattling, little hairs are quivering, and a flood of impulses is charging along our auditory nerves to our brain. Without even trying, we are transforming these impulses into the sensation of hearing, segmenting the sounds into words (remember that the sound stream itself is continuous), identifying the meanings of the words, comprehending the ways in which they are related, making sense out of sentences and strings of sentences, and picking up emotional overtones.

To get some idea of how improbable this is, imagine that you are in a soundproof room looking at an oscilloscope, an electronic device that represents sound waves visually. You are sitting there in silence watching an absolutely chaotic jumble of complex, changing patterns that never pauses for an instant to let you perceive a single shape, and yet you have no trouble at all recognizing what is being said, who is saying it, and how he is feeling today. This is simply asking our eyes to do what our ears do all the time. The raw data are all there, the same raw data that we hear. One thing that computer science is doing for us, incidentally, is highlighting how much we take for granted. It turns out not to be easy to get a very sophisticated computer to do some of the things we do every day without even noticing. It might actually be true in more ways than one that "artificial intelligence is no match for natural stupidity."

The point of this digression is that the internalization of any discipline affords us a freedom that can be attained in no other way. The fullest freedom, the freedom Swedenborg calls *heavenly*, is the freedom that most fully internalizes the world around us. It involves, if you will, an ultimate realism, an openness to whatever is out there with no conflicting desire to shape it to our preferences. There is no sense of being controlled by outside forces for the simple and obvious reason that there is no conflict between those forces and ourselves.

Swedenborg's descriptions of heavenly government follow from this. The people in positions of authority are the people who are most sensitive to others. This leads to the suspicion that our own forms of government are distinguished from each other by the ways in which they handle conflict. If everyone is in agreement, it can be hard to tell which way power is flowing. Swedenborg's heaven could be described as tyranny, since the Lord's will rules absolutely; as anarchy, since no one is forced to do anything; as democracy, since everyone participates in every decision; as capitalism, since there are no restraints in individual initiative; as communism, since there is no sense of exclusive rights; as aristocracy, since the wisest and best bear the most responsibility; or as just about any other system we have devised in our efforts to outwit ourselves. It gives me particular delight to read in Robert's *Rules of Order* that these rules are designed to facilitate the processes of an organization, specifically, to protect the rights of the minority. They are intended, that is, to guarantee that conflict is handled fairly, and Robert specifies that, when they obstruct this intent, they not only may but should be dispensed with.[4] My delight is spiced by the realization the "Robert" was Lieutenant Colonel Henry M. Robert and that this recognition of the limits of the rules was the conclusion of a military mind.

Hellish freedom, as already noted, resembles heavenly freedom in its wholeheartedness; but that is where the resemblance ceases. Hellish freedom is the freedom to be a law unto ourselves, the freedom to believe whatever we feel like believing, no matter what is actually out there. Nobody, but nobody, is going to tell us what to believe or what to do. Each of us is, in effect, god, creator of our own universe, author of our own commandments.

---

4. Henry M. Robert, *Pocket Manual of Rules of Order for Deliberative Assemblies* (Chicago: S. C. Griggs, 1888), 105, 165.

Out of the night that covers me,
Black as the pit from pole to pole,
I thank whatever gods there be
For my unconquerable soul.

It matters not how strait the gate,
How charged with punishment the scroll,
I am the master of my fate,
I am the captain of my soul.[5]

Like the parents in Peck's *People of the Lie*, we regard what we think and say as true simply because it is ours. No other reason is needed. No other reason is admissible, because any other reason might also be useful to someone else. "Ours" is the one claim no one else can share, the one claim over which we have complete control. It is the only safe ground in the universe, and it is as small as we are.

This attitude, obviously, is as unrealistic as the heavenly attitude is realistic. It demands that we screen out everything that challenges it; and, in a hell of like-minded souls, everyone challenges it. It demands that we go against the grain. It is, therefore, an intrinsically self-limiting freedom. Because we are in constant conflict with our (anti?)social environment, we are constantly thwarted. There is nowhere we can turn that we will not meet opposition. We have no "home" where we are

---

5. William Ernest Henley, "Invictus," in *The New Oxford Book of English Verse*, ed. Helen Gardner (New York: Oxford University Press, 1972), 792. Incidentally, this quotation was chosen before Timothy McVeigh chose it as his final statement.

understood, accepted, and welcomed. The most we can say is that we all know and are playing by the same rules.

To put it another way, the only way I can be a law unto myself is to shrink my world down to the space that I can control. That turns out to be an inner space (since others of at least equal strength are competing for the space between us) and, in fact, only a small part of that. I cannot admit to consciousness anything from within or without that claims autonomy—no perception, no thought, no impulse.

How free am I, then? I am absolutely the captain of my soul, the author of my own laws, but I am constrained on every side. By denying the legitimacy of the world around me, the validity of the people around me, I inevitably make myself a minority of one, a prime candidate for crushing defeat. Mikhail Kazachkov described the average Russian, faced with the power of the government, as feeling like an ant in front of a steamroller.[6] That is what hellish freedom makes us, at the same time that it obliges us to believe that we are the steamroller and that the rest of the universe is the ant.

Now we may return to the subject of our here-and-now freedom and our ambivalence toward it. Underlying that ambivalence, I believe, is an instinctive longing for the basic freedom to be who we are, the freedom that is characteristic of both heaven and hell. The trouble is, we have not yet decided who we are, and there is a war going on within us. The heavenly route demands that we let the outside world in, that we allow other people into our minds and hearts. The hellish route demands that we

---

6. "What Ever Happened to the Evil Empire?," op. cit.

shut them out. I'm reminded of a conversation I had with one of our children, aged perhaps four or five. "When you're good, you're so happy, right?" "Yes . . ." "And when you're not good, you're not happy, right?" (Pause) "Isn't there anything in between?"

In fact, Swedenborg is saying, we are in between, but we can't stay there forever. Within the limits of our circumstances, we will tend more and more consistently in one direction or the other. There are all kinds of gradations on the scale, but there is a definite difference between upward and downward, making it far better to start at the bottom and head up than to start at the top and head down. We are headed for unanimity of one kind or the other. That is the inner dimension of our present lives, the geography of the unseen world within us.

Let me put it another way, and begin by saying that we need each other. Our advances in technology, far from making us more independent as individuals, are making us more interdependent. When I was growing up, I doubt that there was anything in the house that my father could not repair. The most sophisticated bit of technology was a cabinet radio. Now, even with information my father knew nothing of, it seems as though there is scarcely anything in the house that I *can* repair. Or to take another example, for a children's sermon recently I used an ordinary can of soup and started listing the people involved in its production. We might start with the farmers and the cooks, but that is only the beginning. There are the administrators of the company; the people who transport the materials; the miners, smelters, and manufacturers who provide the can; the lumberjacks and paper mill workers who provide the labels; the chemists who provide the inks; the label designers—how many people can you pay with $1.19?

We need each other, and if we did not, we would be useless to each other. Why should anyone hire me? I cannot imagine any greater curse than epidemic self-sufficiency, the sentence of absolute irrelevance, utter and ineluctable insignificance.

The complexity of the fabric of our interdependence is quite marvelous. It is, at its best, a striking example of that excellence that is attained when the components of a system are "distinguishably different, and yet united." When I find my place in that fabric, my needs for autonomy, for individuality, are no longer in conflict with my needs for inclusion. The greatest contribution I can make to human society is to be my authentic self. The best way to be my authentic self is to make my greatest contribution to human society. That, for me, is what freedom is all about.

Perhaps, then, the simplest way to express a Swedenborgian response to the theodicy question is to say that here and now we are free to choose heaven or hell and that, after death, we will be free to stay in hell just as long as we want to. Nothing in the divine will, nothing in the structure of the moral-spiritual universe will compel us not to want to stay there. The only pressure to change will be that pressure of reality we have skilled ourselves in resisting and denying.

There is another dimension of this that I have not found dealt with in my limited reading, namely, the matter of our own relationship to eternity. One of our daughters once confessed that the idea of living forever troubled her—not specifically the idea of eternity in hell, apparently, but simply the idea of her life going on and on forever. I doubt that I am the only person who has not at one time or another felt the appeal of the notion of falling asleep and never waking up.

Most of the time, though, our anticipations of the future are sized to fit our circumstances. We look forward to graduation or to marriage or to the kids growing up and leaving home or to retirement. We look forward to the end of a hard day or a long trip or a cold winter or a boring conversation. We look forward to putting the last coat of varnish on the dining room table, sewing the last seam on a blouse, drying the last of the dishes.

That is, when we are engaged in something we feel is worthwhile, we are content within the temporal space which that something delimits. I think of heavenly eternal life not as looking ahead into an endless future but as a constant fascination with the present. There is a goal in sight, a relationship to foster, something to learn, someone to love. There is the joy of self-forgetfulness.

When we are involved in something painful, on the other hand, we look forward to the end of that episode. I find it quite believable that people in hell are often ready to mend their ways tomorrow, to turn over a new leaf as soon as the time is right. I find it quite believable that hope could spring eternal, especially in people totally convinced (even against overwhelming evidence to the contrary) of their own importance. The gratifications of self-indulgence can be quite persuasive if we want them to.

In a sense, what I am urging is that we shift the

argument from the cosmic and theoretical to the personal, because Swedenborg's hell is a personal one. It is a little like shifting the focus from national policy on homelessness to case-working with homeless individuals. The policy may satisfy all kinds of theoretical or statistical demands, but it should ultimately stand or fall on its actual effectiveness in individual cases. Rather than globalize about the eternity of hell, then, we might better posit an individual's deciding to leave hell. Surely, the argument goes, sooner or later anyone is bound to realize that this kind of life is self-defeating. Sooner or later, the suffering and the brutality will get through.

The main trouble I have with this is that it represents no change whatever in the essential self-centeredness of our hypothetical individual. If that individual were to look at someone else with a trace of sympathy, that would represent a change. As it is, this individual is still wholly wrapped up in her own suffering, all the more wrapped up in it the more overwhelming it becomes. Far from awakening sympathies, the suffering serves to reinforce the conviction that everyone else is the enemy. There is convincing evidence that our own prisons reinforce criminal patterns of behavior more than they rehabilitate. Can we really believe that intensifying and prolonging the punishment will work any better? If we remove from the penal system everyone who actually wants to help, if we remove every trace of concern for the inmates, will that bring about changes of heart? Where is the evidence?

The closest thing to a favorable outcome of this theory of the benefits of punishment is a picture of an individual beaten into submission by pain, and this I find wholly inconsistent with any notion of a loving God. If it is the nature of love to feel the joy of another as joy in oneself, then it is the longing of love to feel love in the other, and what love could there be in the heart of a man so utterly defeated? "Thanks, I needed that?"

Again, the Johannine epistles (1 John 4:20–21) insist on the oneness of the two great commandments.

> Those who say, "I love God" and hate their brothers or sisters are liars; for those who do not love a brother or sister whom they have seen cannot love God whom they have not seen. The commandment we have from him is this: those who love God must love their brothers and sisters also.

What this is saying is, so to speak, that we define the word *love* by the way we treat each other; and a corollary of this is that our own experiences of love are the basis of our "definitions" of God's love. On this basis, I would urge that we take seriously the concept of "tough love," so practically advocated by AlAnon. Effective love for the alcoholic—and any genuine love includes an intent to be effective—means refusing to rescue him. The greatest hope for recovery lies in his being faced with the consequences of his addiction, and rescue attempts will serve only to postpone that confrontation.

This fits both with Swedenborg's insistence that love needs wisdom and with the view already expressed that, in the here and now, we are free to change the basic direction of our lives. Again, I find this picture of love, wisdom, and freedom exquisitely realized in the design of a world in which reality constantly presses us toward sanity but with enough ambiguity that we can construct worlds to our own liking out of the available material.

There is one further matter that cannot responsibly be passed over in silence. While I hope that the mechanism of judgment has been made clear and can stand as consistent with a loving God, the timing of that judgment is another matter. In a Swedenborgian view presented earlier in this chapter, the transition from a physical to a spiritual world entails the transition from the freedom to choose between heaven and hell to the freedom to be wholly in the one or the other, and this is a critical transition. Hamlet looked at his hated uncle, in prayer, and declined to send him to that spiritual world when he was at his most devout. Thornton Wilder's *The Bridge of San Luis Rey* represents an earnest attempt to wrestle with the issue through the medium of fiction, reconstructing the lives of individuals killed in the collapse of a footbridge and coming to the conclusion that, for each one, the time of death was ideal.

There are doubtless serious theological explorations of this theme, and it may be significant that none has caught my attention, that the two instances in the previous paragraph come from the world of fiction. As far as I can see, there is simply no way to prove that anyone has or has not died at the time best for his or her spiritual future. It may strain credulity to believe that with all the uncertainties we face, every single individual who has died of natural or unnatural causes has died at the optimum moment. It may strain credulity almost as much as the dogma that no two snowflakes are alike.

epiLogue

The cartoonist Peter Arno had the observer's eye. One of his cartoons showed an obviously depressed man pouring out his troubles to a sympathetic bartender. The caption: "My wife understands me." Ogden Nash wrote a poem about a mind-reading husband who thoughtfully anticipated his wife's every desire. She finally poisoned him because she could not stand being perpetually understood.

Let's face it, personal, intimate transparency is no small price to pay for admission to heaven. But let's also face the fact that there can be no real heaven without it. As long as we feel we have to guard ourselves against discovery, we cannot be at peace, and we have no rest from the hell of self-concealment. Or to put it affirmatively, wouldn't it be wonderful not to have to pretend any more? Wouldn't it be bliss to know that the affection that surrounded us was based on understanding and not on some illusion that might collapse at any moment?

At the heart of Swedenborg's view of heaven and hell is a single idea of extraordinary depth, power, and simplicity: genuine love, and only genuine love, is truly clear-sighted. Anything else distorts our vision. Infatuation may be blind, lust may be blind, possessiveness may be blind, but not love. That is the truth behind Kazachkov's conviction that evil always lies. It lies because, as perfect love casts out fear, so fear casts out love, and with it clarity of vision. Again, that is what Helen Keller grasped so clearly and said so well:

> As selfishness and complaint pervert and cloud the mind, so love with its joy clears and sharpens the vision. It gives the delicacy of perception to see wonders in what before seemed dull and trivial. It replenishes the springs of inspiration, and its joy sends a new river of lifelike blood through the matter-clogged faculties.[1]

Love is ultimately realistic because it is not afraid to understand. If I genuinely care about you, I do not want illusions or pretense. I want to know where it hurts and where it does not, because otherwise my best intentions will not guard me against doing you harm. Similarly, I do not want you to have illusions about me, to waste your affections on some imaginary being cobbled together out of what I see as my redeeming qualities.

---

1. *The Open Door*, op. cit., 35.

For me, this relationship between love and truth utterly demolishes any view of God that would have divine judgment at odds with divine mercy, divine truth at odds with divine love. We are loved because we are known and understood, and we are known and understood because we are loved. Love does not distort God's vision. Swedenborg began his first published theological overview with a chapter on "Good and Truth," stating that there was nothing more necessary for us than to know what they are and how they relate to each other.[2] After years of mild frustration at his failing to offer a definition of either term, I have finally focused on the immense significance of what he does say, namely, that they are one in Deity and should become one in us. Genuine love (which for Swedenborg is virtually synonymous with "the good") can be defined as the longing for truth and genuine truth, as the manifestation of love.

Further, loving and being loved, understanding and being understood, are inseparable. We can hide ourselves from others only by hiding them from ourselves. Evil confines us to a universe of our own creation, and we are pathetically poor, petty creators. True human community is surpassingly lovely, well worth the price of admission. Hell is pathetic primarily by contrast, pathetic in heaven's light, although not in its own. Perhaps the theodicy question needs to be turned around. How do I manage to rationalize my selfishness in the face of the love and wisdom of the Creator so eloquently witnessed by the beauty and sanity of true human community?

---

2. *The New Jerusalem and Its Heavenly Doctrine* §§11–19.

biBLiogRaphy of woRks by emanueL sweɒeNborg

Apocalypse Explained. 6 vols. Translated by John Whitehead. 2nd ed. West Chester, Pa.: The Swedenborg Foundation, 1994–1998.

Apocalypse Revealed. 2 vols. Translated by John Whitehead. 2nd ed. West Chester, Pa.: The Swedenborg Foundation, 1997.

Arcana Coelestia. 12 vols. Translated by John Clowes. Rvd. John F. Potts. 2nd ed. West Chester, Pa.: The Swedenborg Foundation, 1995–1998. The first volume of this work is also available under the title *Heavenly Secrets.*

Charity: The Practice of Neighborliness. Translated by William F. Wunsch. Ed. William R. Woofenden. West Chester, Pa.: The Swedenborg Foundation, 1995.

Conjugial Love. Translated by Samuel S. Warren. Rvd. Louis Tafel. 2nd ed. West Chester, Pa.: The Swedenborg Foundation, 1998. This volume is also available under the title *Love in Marriage*, translated by David Gladish, 1992.

Divine Love and Wisdom. Translated by John C. Ager. 2nd ed. West Chester, Pa.: The Swedenborg Foundation, 1995. This volume is also available in a translation by George F. Dole.

Divine Providence. Translated by William Wunsch. 2nd ed. West Chester, Pa.: The Swedenborg Foundation, 1996.

Four Doctrines. Translated by John F. Potts. 2nd ed. West Chester, Pa.: The Swedenborg Foundation, 1997.

Heaven and Hell. Translated by John C. Ager. 2nd ed. West Chester, Pa.: The Swedenborg Foundation, 1995.

————. Translated by George F. Dole. The New Century Edition of the Works of Emanuel Swedenborg. West Chester, Pa.: The Swedenborg Foundation, 2000.

The Heavenly City. Translated by Lee Woofenden. West Chester, Pa.: The Swedenborg Foundation, 1993.

Journal of Dreams. Translated by J. J. G. Wilkinson. Introduction by Wilson Van Dusen. New York: The Swedenborg Foundation, 1986. See also *Swedenborg's Dream Diary.*

The Last Judgment in Retrospect. Translated by and edited by George F. Dole. West Chester, Pa.: The Swedenborg Foundation, 1996.

Miscellaneous Theological Works. Translated by John Whitehead. 2nd ed. West Chester, Pa.: The Swedenborg Foundation, 1996. This volume includes *The New Jerusalem and Its Heavenly Doctrine, Earths in the Universe,* and *The Last Judgment and Babylon Destroyed,* among others.

Posthumous Theological Works. 2 vols. Translated by John Whitehead. 2nd ed. West Chester, Pa.: The Swedenborg Foundation, 1996. These volumes include the autobiographical and theological extracts from Swedenborg's letters, additions to *True Christian Religion, The Doctrine of Charity, The Precepts of the Decalogue,* and collected minor works, among others.

Swedenborg's Dream Diary. Edited by Lars Bergquist. Translated by Anders Hallengren. West Chester, Pa.: The Swedenborg Foundation, 2001. See also *Journal of Dreams.*

True Christian Religion. 2 vols. Translated by John C. Ager. West Chester, Pa.: The Swedenborg Foundation, 1996.

Worship and Love of God. Translated by Alfred H. Stroh and Frank Sewall. 2nd ed. West Chester, Pa.: The Swedenborg Foundation, 1996.